HOUSE
WARMING
PATCH
WORK

Housewarming Patchwork
First published in the United States in 2013 by Interweave Press

Interweave Press LLC,
A division of F+W Media Inc.
201 East Fourth Street
Loveland, CO 80537
interweave.com

Copyright ©Yoko Saito / NIHON VOGUE-SHA 2005
156 Original Patchwork Designs
Originally published in Japanese language by Nihon Vogue Co., LTD.
English language rights, translation & production by World Book Media, LLC
Email: info@worldbookmedia.com

Photographer: Akinori Miyashita, Kana Watanabe
Translation: Kyoko Matthews
English-language editor: Lindsay Fair

Library of Congress
Cataloging-in-Publication Data not available at time of printing

ISBN-13: 978-1596688193

Printed in China
10 9 8 7 6 5 4 3 2 1

HOUSE WARMING PATCH WORK

YOKO SAITO

78 original motifs and
10 projects

CONTENTS

Introduction

This book celebrates and commemorates my 30 years as a patchwork quilter. I was first attracted to patchwork quilting when I happened across a photograph of a simple, yet beautiful traditional American quilt in a magazine. I found the practice of combining small scraps of fabric to create an endless variety of designs so appealing and was inspired by the history behind traditional patchwork motifs.

Over the years, I have greatly enjoyed designing patterns that offer fresh interpretations of traditional motifs. When I am inspired by an antique quilt, I begin my design process by drawing out the pattern. Then, I will often sharpen angles and slant lines to make the design slightly off balance and add visual interest. Thousands of different motifs exist today because quilters have rearranged traditional patterns and created their own unique variations.

When creating motifs from scratch, I use a ruler and graph paper to chart out a design. Faced with a blank sheet of paper, new designs begin to appear before my eyes! I am inspired by the everyday objects that surround me: houses, animals, flowers...even sewing tools!

Once I have a pattern, I love selecting my fabrics. I put a great amount of effort into choosing the right fabric for each element of the design. It's amazing how a striped fabric can replicate tree bark so realistically or a woven fabric can mimic the texture of a basket so perfectly.

I hope the designs featured in this book inspire you to sew a few blocks using your favorite fabrics. Join the blocks together into a quilt, or use them to create any of the fun projects included in this book. You may even be inspired to create your own original patchwork designs!

Yoko Saito

How to Use This Book

Each block design includes a full-size photograph, a full-size template, and a construction steps diagram. To make a block, cut out all the patchwork pieces, then sew the pieces together following the process illustrated by the construction steps. The following guide shows you how the block instructions are formatted in this book and includes some general tips for creating the blocks.

Appliqué

Outline stitch (1 strand)

SELECTING YOUR FABRIC

- ❖ Scrap fabric is used for all blocks, so the block instructions do not include a materials list.
- ❖ When selecting your fabric, opt for prints and patterns that correspond with the motif. For example, I often use wood grain fabric for trees and plaid woven fabric for baskets.
- ❖ The photographs of each block are full-size, excluding seam allowances. The finished size for most blocks is a 3½" (9 cm) square.

The designs in this book were created using metric measurements. Any measurements noted in inches within the book are conversions of the metric measurements. For the greatest accuracy, use the metric version of all measurements.

CUTTING THE BLOCKS

- ❖ The templates in this book are full-size, unless otherwise noted. Using the template will produce a 3½" (9 cm) square finished block.
- ❖ The templates can be enlarged or reduced as desired. Each template is printed on a grid of ³⁄₁₆" (0.5 cm) squares. Use this measurement as your scale when resizing.
- ❖ The templates do not include seam allowance. When cutting your fabric, add ¼" (0.6 cm) seam allowance around each patchwork piece.
- ❖ When adjacent patchwork pieces are divided with a gray line on the template, use the same fabric for both pieces.
- ❖ Pink lines on the block template indicate appliqué and embroidery.

CONSTRUCTION STEPS

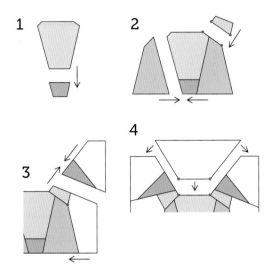

SEWING FROM EDGE TO EDGE

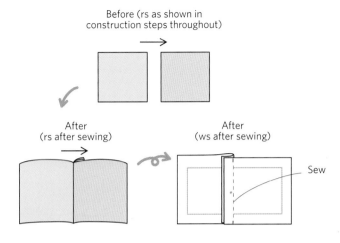

Sew from edge to edge and press the seam allowance in the direction indicated by the arrow.

SEWING THE BLOCKS

- ❖ All of the blocks in this book are created with basic patchwork sewing. Some of the blocks also incorporate appliqué and embroidery, which are done once the block has been pieced together.
- ❖ The numbers indicate the order in which the patchwork pieces are sewn together to form the block. Follow the recommended sewing order for best results.
- ❖ Always sew with ¼" (0.6 cm) seam allowance, unless otherwise noted.
- ❖ Unless otherwise noted, sew the patchwork pieces together from edge to edge. Backstitch at both the beginning and end of each seam.
- ❖ The red dots indicate to start or stop sewing at the seam allowance, rather than from edge to edge. This technique is used to set pieces into each other.
- ❖ The arrows indicate the direction to press the seam allowance. The seam allowance should always be pressed in the direction that makes it least visible from the right side. Use the arrows as a guide; however, you may need to make adjustments based on the color or thickness of your fabric.

USING THE RED DOTS:
How to Start and Stop Sewing at the Seam Allowance

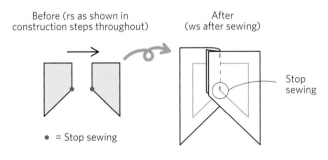

● = Stop sewing

Stop sewing at the red dot and press the seam allowance in the direction indicated by the arrow. Seam allowance will not be pictured in the construction steps.

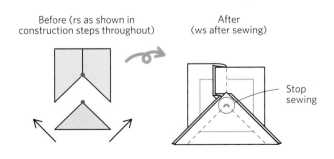

1 Teapot

Enjoy tea time while quilting this energizing design. I used a muted floral print for the teapot to simulate subtly patterned china.

CONSTRUCTION STEPS

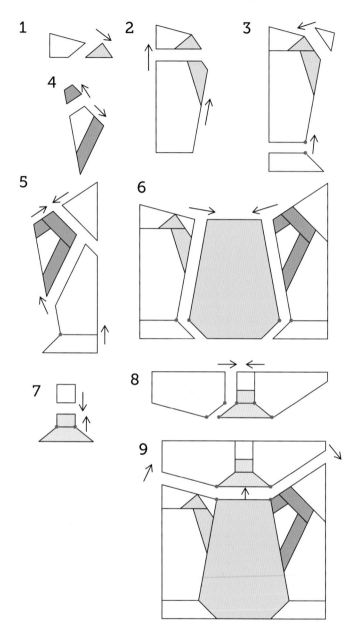

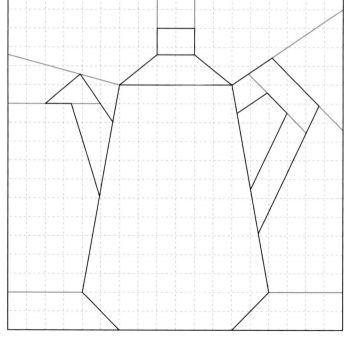

- ✤ When cutting your fabric, add ¼" (0.6 cm) seam allowance around each patchwork piece. Seam allowance is not pictured in the construction steps.
- ✤ When adjacent pieces are divided with a gray line, use the same fabric.
- ✤ Always press the seam allowance in the direction indicated by the arrows.
- ✤ The • marks to stop sewing at the seam allowance.

CONSTRUCTION STEPS

1

2

3

4

5

6

7

8

9

Outline stitch

Create a whole tea set by using coordinating fabrics for this teacup plus the teapot and sugar bowl designs featured in this collection. Embroider a bit of steam rising from the cup to add a special detail.

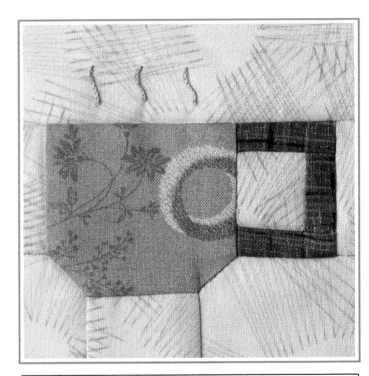

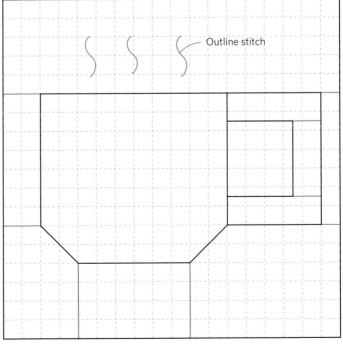

Outline stitch

❖ When cutting your fabric, add ¼" (0.6 cm) seam allowance around each patchwork piece. Seam allowance is not pictured in the construction steps.

❖ When adjacent pieces are divided with a gray line, use the same fabric.

❖ Always press the seam allowance in the direction indicated by the arrows.

❖ The • marks to stop sewing at the seam allowance.

3 Sugar Bowl

Combine patchwork and appliqué techniques to create this sweet sugar bowl. Experiment with fabric print and consider adding embroidery or additional appliqué designs for a one-of-a-kind block...the possibilities are endless!

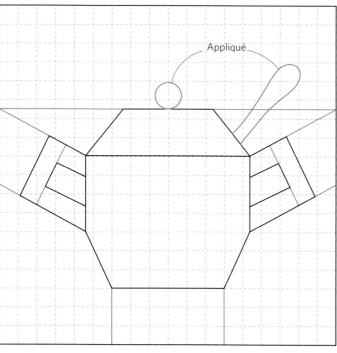

Appliqué

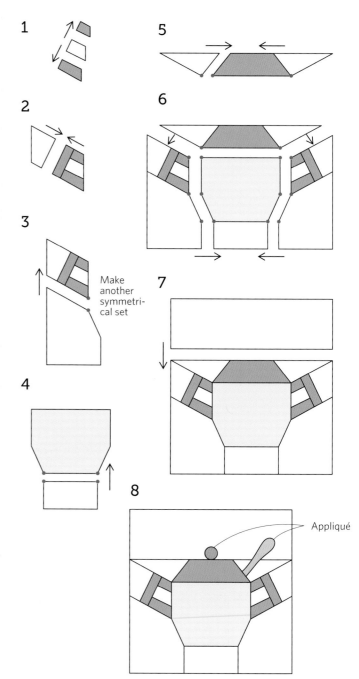

1

2

3

Make another symmetrical set

4

5

6

7

8

Appliqué

❖ When cutting your fabric, add ¼" (0.6 cm) seam allowance around each patchwork piece. Seam allowance is not pictured in the construction steps.

❖ When adjacent pieces are divided with a gray line, use the same fabric.

❖ Always press the seam allowance in the direction indicated by the arrows.

❖ The • marks to stop sewing at the seam allowance.

CONSTRUCTION STEPS

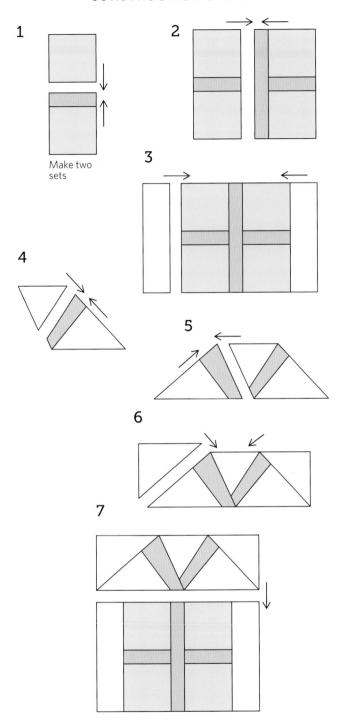

1

Make two sets

2

3

4

5

6

7

With its fun wrapping paper and pretty bow, who wouldn't be tempted to open this present? Use this block for a wide variety of occasions by changing your fabric choices. Use a red and green color scheme for Christmas designs or use brightly colored fabrics for birthday projects.

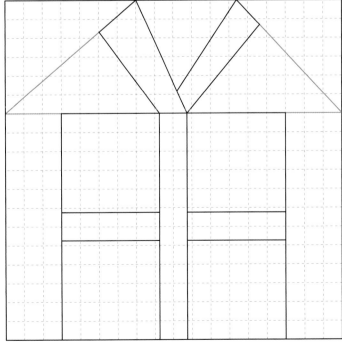

- ❖ When cutting your fabric, add ¼" (0.6 cm) seam allowance around each patchwork piece. Seam allowance is not pictured in the construction steps.
- ❖ When adjacent pieces are divided with a gray line, use the same fabric.
- ❖ Always press the seam allowance in the direction indicated by the arrows.

5 Mitten

This adorable winter necessity is made with simple patchwork quilting. I chose a plaid fabric for the main part of the mitten to create the look of wool and a thin stripe for the ribbing. This block works well for the Business Card Holder project shown on page 16.

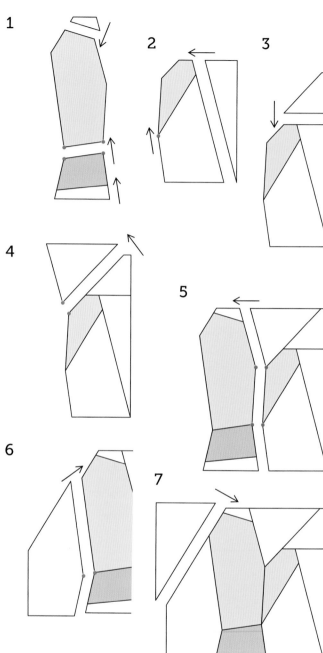

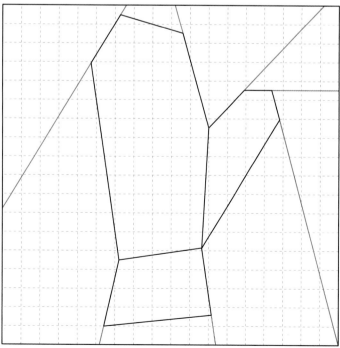

❖ When cutting your fabric, add ¼" (0.6 cm) seam allowance around each patchwork piece. Seam allowance is not pictured in the construction steps.

❖ When adjacent pieces are divided with a gray line, use the same fabric.

❖ Always press the seam allowance in the direction indicated by the arrows.

❖ The • marks to stop sewing at the seam allowance.

CONSTRUCTION STEPS

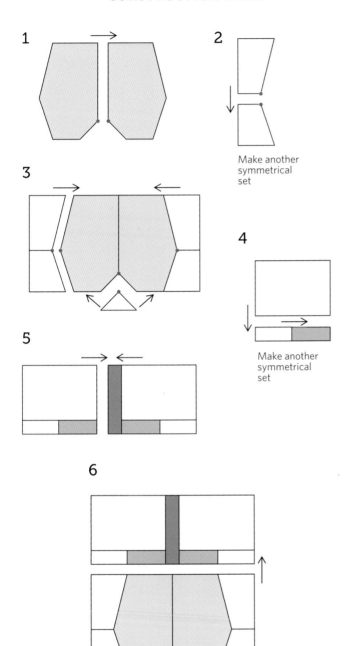

1

2

Make another symmetrical set

3

4

Make another symmetrical set

5

6

- When cutting your fabric, add ¼" (0.6 cm) seam allowance around each patchwork piece. Seam allowance is not pictured in the construction steps.
- When adjacent pieces are divided with a gray line, use the same fabric.
- Always press the seam allowance in the direction indicated by the arrows.
- The • marks to stop sewing at the seam allowance.

6 Harvest Basket

This block features a uniquely-shaped basket perfect for picking fruits and vegetables. For this design, I chose realistic prints to replicate the texture of an actual woven basket. This block is used in the Business Card Holder project shown on page 16.

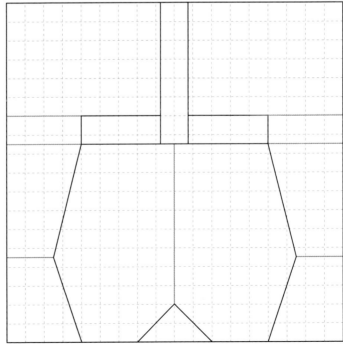

Business Card Holder

Create a one-of-a-kind card holder that will stand out from the crowd. Make the cover, then simply insert the plastic sleeves. I used the Harvest Basket and Mitten blocks because I felt the small scale of the project suited these charming designs, but feel free to use whichever block you like best.

MATERIALS FOR BUSINESS CARD HOLDER

Patchwork fabric: Assorted scraps

Top fabric: 6" × 9¾" (15 × 25 cm) beige print

Backing fabric: 6¾" × 8¾" (17 × 22 cm)

Lining fabric: 6" × 23⅝" (15 × 60 cm)

Interfacing: 6¾" × 8¾" (17 × 22 cm)

Hook-and-loop tape: 5⁄16" × 7⁄16" (0.8 × 1.2 cm)

Button: One ¼" (0.6 cm) diameter button

Card holder: One 2¾" × 4" (7 × 10 cm) set of plastic sleeves

CUTTING INSTRUCTIONS

Seam allowance is not included. Add ¼" (0.6 cm) seam allowance to all piece edges.

Trace and cut out the Block #5 or Block #6 template on page 14 or 15. Using the template, cut the patchwork pieces out of scrap fabric.

Cut out the following pieces, which do not have templates, according to the measurements below:

❖ **A (cut 2):** ⅜" × 3⅛" (1 × 8 cm) of top fabric
❖ **Back:** 3⅛" × 4¼" (8 × 11 cm) of top fabric
❖ **Tab (cut 2):** ⅜" × 1³⁄16" (1 × 3 cm) of scrap fabric
❖ **Pocket (cut 2):** 4¼" × 5½" (11 × 14 cm) of lining fabric
❖ **Lining:** 4¼" × 6¼" (11 × 16 cm) of lining fabric

LAYOUT DIAGRAM

TOP

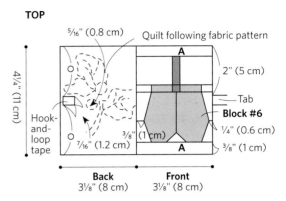

Back 3⅛" (8 cm)   **Front** 3⅛" (8 cm)

LINING

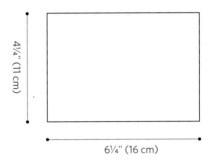

4¼" (11 cm)

6¼" (16 cm)

POCKET

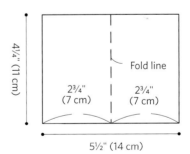

4¼" (11 cm)

Fold line

2¾" (7 cm)   2¾" (7 cm)

5½" (14 cm)

TAB

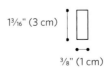

1³⁄16" (3 cm)

⅜" (1 cm)

❖ Stitch in the ditch along patchwork pieces.
❖ Sew using ¼" (0.6 cm) seam allowance, unless otherwise noted.

MAKE THE CARD HOLDER

1. Follow the instructions on pages 14 or 15 to make Block #5 or Block #6.

2. To make the front, sew one piece A to the top and bottom of the block. Attach the back.

3. Cut the interfacing and backing slightly larger than the assembled top. Layer the top, interfacing, and backing. Stitch in the ditch along all patchwork pieces. Quilt, following the fabric pattern, then quilt remaining areas as desired.

4. On the right side, sew one piece of hook-and-loop tape to the back.

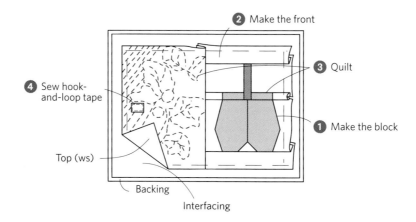

2 Make the front

3 Quilt

1 Make the block

4 Sew hook-and-loop tape

Top (ws)

Backing

Interfacing

MAKE THE TAB

1. Sew remaining piece of hook-and-loop tape to one tab.

2. Align tabs with right sides together and sew along three sides. Trim the corner seam allowances at angles.

3. Turn right side out. Topstitch tab along edges.

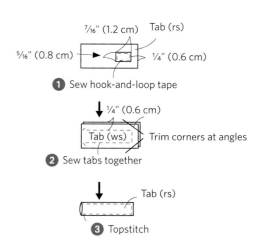

7/16" (1.2 cm)   Tab (rs)

5/16" (0.8 cm)   1/4" (0.6 cm)

1 Sew hook-and-loop tape

1/4" (0.6 cm)

Tab (ws)   Trim corners at angles

2 Sew tabs together

Tab (rs)

3 Topstitch

MAKE THE POCKETS

1. Fold each pocket in half with right sides facing out. Baste.

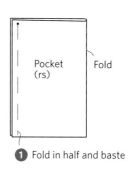

Pocket (rs)   Fold

1 Fold in half and baste

ATTACH THE POCKETS, TAB, AND LINING

1. On the right side, baste the tab to the front.

2. Layer the pockets and top. Baste together around the three sides of each pocket.

3. Layer the lining and top with right sides together. Sew together around all sides, leaving a 2" (5 cm) opening. Trim excess interfacing and backing seam allowance. Turn right side out through the opening.

4. Fold in the opening seam allowance and slip-stitch closed.

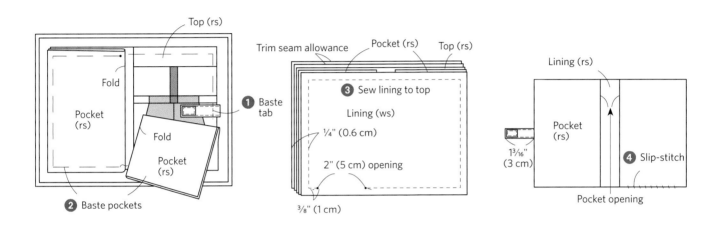

FINISH THE CARD HOLDER

1. On the right side, attach a button to the tab.

2. Insert the plastic sleeves into the pockets.

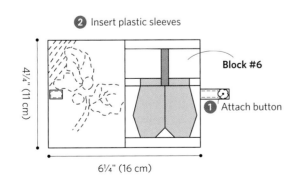

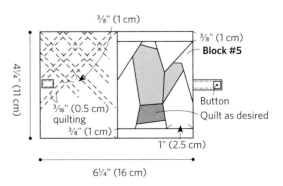

7 Clover

The four-leaf clover is a well-known symbol of good luck. When selecting fabric, I opted for a green and white print and created the clover's characteristic white circle by fussy cutting the leaves. Hand-dyed fabrics, such as batiks, are ideal for this motif.

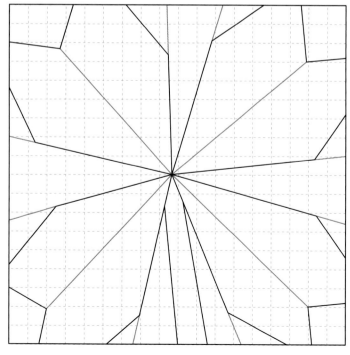

1

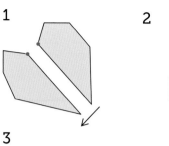

2

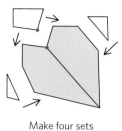

Make four sets

3

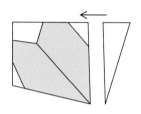

4

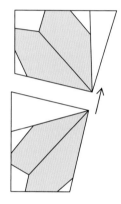

5

6

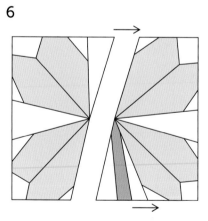

* When cutting your fabric, add ¼" (0.6 cm) seam allowance around each patchwork piece. Seam allowance is not pictured in the construction steps.
* When adjacent pieces are divided with a gray line, use the same fabric.
* Always press the seam allowance in the direction indicated by the arrows.
* The • marks to stop sewing at the seam allowance.

CONSTRUCTION STEPS

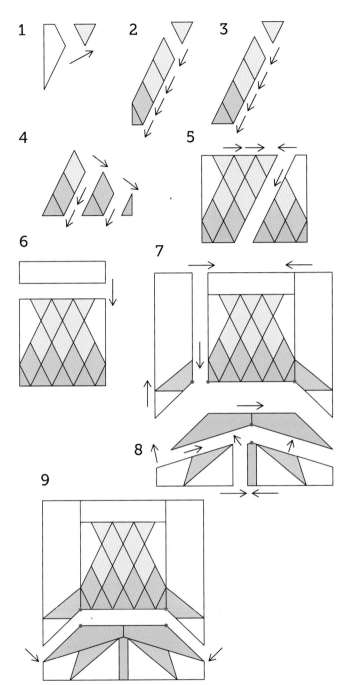

8 Thistle

The thistle plant is characterized by prickly thorns, which protect a fragile flower. This block is composed of sharply angled green thorns and small, diamond-shaped pink petals. For added dimension, I chose a printed background fabric, which represents seeds floating on the wind.

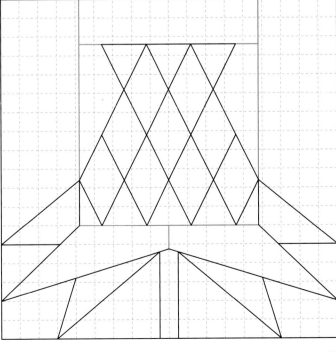

✤ When cutting your fabric, add ¼" (0.6 cm) seam allowance around each patchwork piece. Seam allowance is not pictured in the construction steps.

✤ When adjacent pieces are divided with a gray line, use the same fabric.

✤ Always press the seam allowance in the direction indicated by the arrows.

✤ The • marks to stop sewing at the seam allowance.

9 Flower Basket

Historically, baskets have always been a popular quilting motif as they symbolize the home. They are also a personal favorite—I collect baskets of all shapes and sizes. This classic design utilizes small triangles to create both basket and flowers.

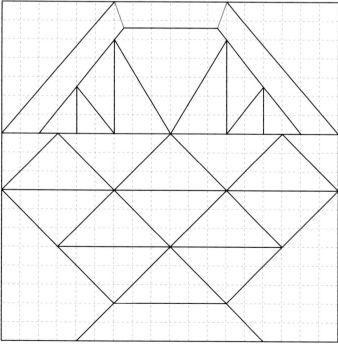

CONSTRUCTION STEPS

1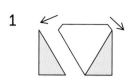

2 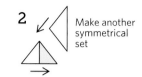 Make another symmetrical set

3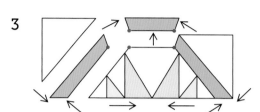

4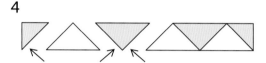

5

6

7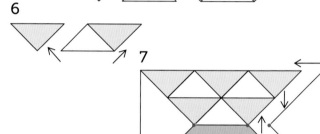

8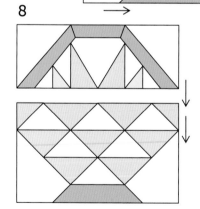

✢ When cutting your fabric, add ¼" (0.6 cm) seam allowance around each patchwork piece. Seam allowance is not pictured in the construction steps.

✢ When adjacent pieces are divided with a gray line, use the same fabric.

✢ Always press the seam allowance in the direction indicated by the arrows.

✢ The • marks to stop sewing at the seam allowance.

10 Nantucket Basket

This design was inspired by the traditional baskets of Nantucket, a small island off the coast of Cape Cod. I recommend using plaid or checkered fabrics to create the appearance of a basket weave.

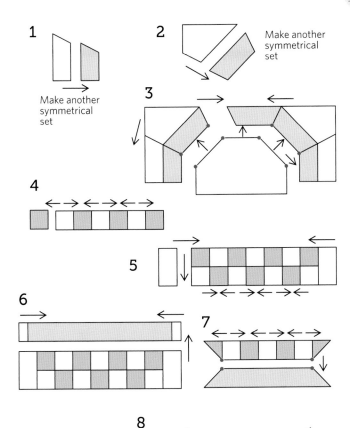

1

Make another symmetrical set

2

Make another symmetrical set

3

4

5

6

7

8

9

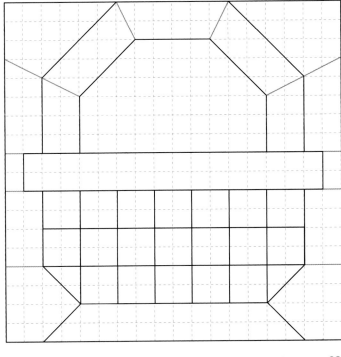

* When cutting your fabric, add ¼" (0.6 cm) seam allowance around each patchwork piece. Seam allowance is not pictured in the construction steps.
* When adjacent pieces are divided with a gray line, use the same fabric.
* Always press the seam allowance in the direction indicated by the arrows.
* The • marks to stop sewing at the seam allowance.

11 Oval Basket

This oval basket is a very versatile design. In this block, I fussy cut and appliquéd print flowers, but fruit or vegetable prints would also work well. This basket design is used in the Water Bottle Tote project shown on page 26, where it is embellished with embroidered flowers.

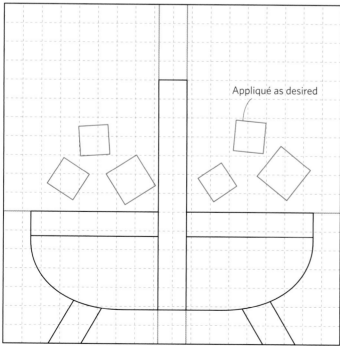

Appliqué as desired

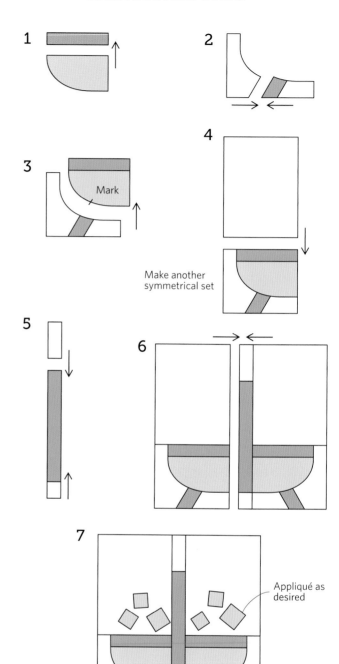

1

2

3   Mark

4   Make another symmetrical set

5

6

7   Appliqué as desired

❖ When cutting your fabric, add ¼" (0.6 cm) seam allowance around each patchwork piece. Seam allowance is not pictured in the construction steps.

❖ When adjacent pieces are divided with a gray line, use the same fabric.

❖ Always press the seam allowances in the direction indicated by the arrows.

CONSTRUCTION STEPS

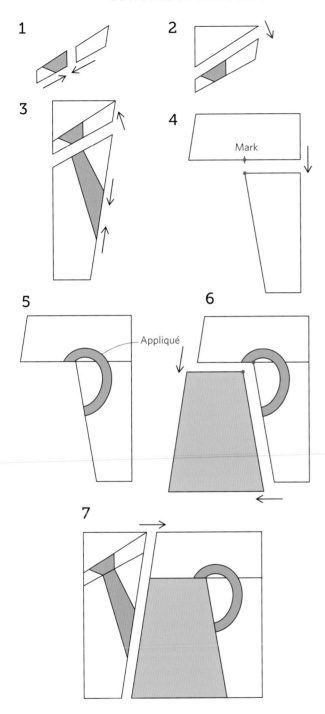

12 Watering Can

This pattern features the simple silhouette of an old-fashioned tin watering can. The curved handle is appliquéd, while the rest of the can is made with patchwork. This block is used in the Water Bottle Tote project shown on page 26, where it is filled with appliquéd and embroidered flowers.

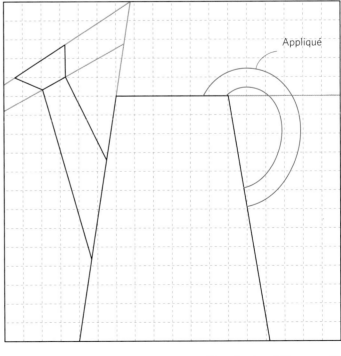

- When cutting your fabric, add ¼" (0.6 cm) seam allowance around each patchwork piece. Seam allowance is not pictured in the construction steps.
- When adjacent pieces are divided with a gray line, use the same fabric.
- Always press the seam allowances in the direction indicated by the arrows.
- The • marks to stop sewing at the seam allowance.

Water Bottle Tote

This beautiful case will transform a boring plastic bottle into a work of art. To create this unique project, sew the Oval Basket and Watering Can blocks, then embellish with a combination of appliqué and embroidery. When selecting your fabric, look for a water-resistant material for the lining, so you'll be able to store an ice-cold bottle inside.

Instructions on page 28

MATERIALS FOR WATER BOTTLE TOTE

Patchwork and appliqué fabric: Assorted scraps

Top fabrics #1 and #2: Two 9¾" × 9¾" (25 × 25 cm) beige flower prints

Bottom fabric: 6" × 6" (15 × 15 cm) brown checkered fabric

Backing fabric: 9¾" × 21¾" (25 × 55 cm)

Lining fabric: 9¾" × 21¾" (25 × 55 cm) water-resistant fabric

Binding: One 1⅜" × 15¾" (3.5 × 40 cm) beige checkered bias strip

Batting: 9¾" × 21¾" (25 × 55 cm)

Handle: 15¾" (40 cm) of ¾" (2 cm) wide nylon webbing tape

Embroidery floss: 6-strand embroidery floss in black, white, green, khaki, yellow, and off-white

CUTTING INSTRUCTIONS

Seam allowance is not included. Add ¼" (0.6 cm) seam allowance to all piece edges.

Trace and cut out the template on Pattern Sheet A and the Block #11 and #12 templates on pages 24 and 25. Cut out the pieces following the instructions listed on the templates.

Cut out the following pieces, which do not have templates, according to the measurements below:

❖ **Gusset (cut 4):** 1½" × 8" (4 x 20 cm) of top fabric #2
❖ **A:** 3 1/16" × 3½" (7.8 × 9 cm) of top fabric #1
❖ **B:** 1¼" × 3½" (3.2 × 9 cm) of scrap fabric
❖ **Bottom:** 3⅛" × 3½" (8 × 9 cm) of bottom fabric

LAYOUT DIAGRAM

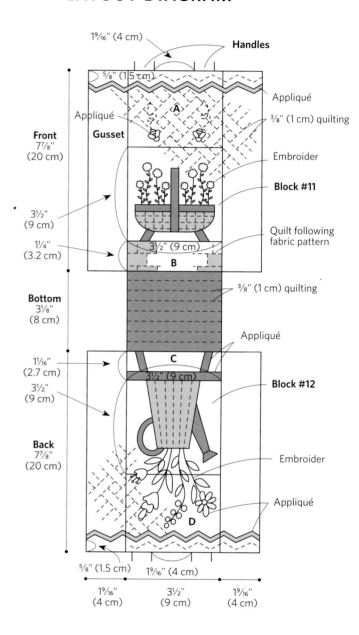

❖ Stitch in the ditch around all appliqué pieces.
❖ Sew using ¼" (0.6 cm) seam allowance, unless otherwise noted.

MAKE THE BAG

1. Follow the instructions on pages 24 and 25 to make Block #11 and Block #12.

2. To make the front, sew pieces A and B to Block #11, then sew a gusset on each side. To make the back, sew pieces C and D to Block #12, then sew a gusset on each side.

3. Appliqué the zigzag design on both the front and back. Note: The zigzag pattern will connect when the front and back are sewn together. Appliqué and embroider the bees and flowers on the front using the template on Pattern Sheet A. Appliqué and embroider the flowers and stand on the back.

4. Make the top by sewing the bottom to both the front and back, starting and stopping at the seam allowances.

5. Cut the batting and backing slightly larger than the assembled top. Layer the top, batting, and backing. Baste, then quilt using the template on Pattern Sheet A. Stitch in the ditch around all appliqué pieces.

6. Fold the top in half so the front and back are aligned with right sides together. Sew together along lower sides using 2⅜" (6 cm) long seams.

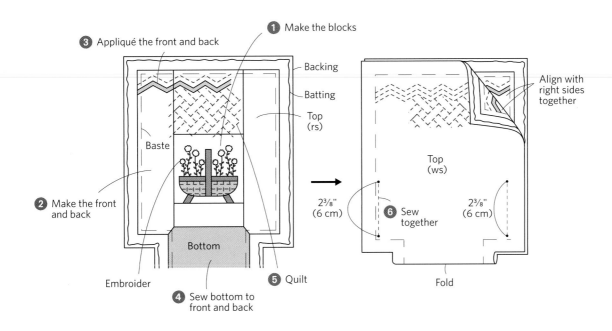

MAKE THE LINING

1 Cut out the lining in the shape of the assembled bag. Fold the lining in half with right sides together and sew along the lower sides using 2⅜" (6 cm) long seams, following the same process used for the top.

2 Layer the lining and top and sew together along the upper sides. Press the seam allowances open. Trim the batting and backing seam allowances to ¼" (0.6 cm).

3 Align the top gussets with the lining gussets and sew together along the bottom. Trim the batting and backing seam allowances to ¼" (0.6 cm). Turn right side out.

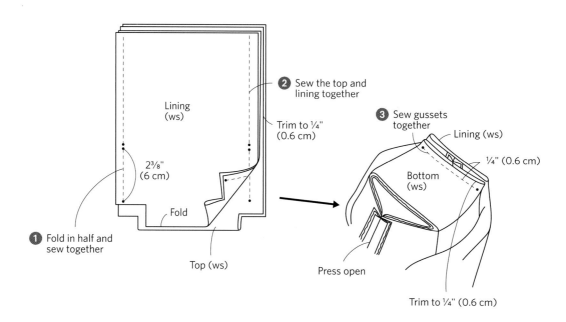

Lining (ws)

2 Sew the top and lining together

Trim to ¼" (0.6 cm)

2⅜" (6 cm)

1 Fold in half and sew together

Fold

Top (ws)

3 Sew gussets together

Lining (ws)

¼" (0.6 cm)

Bottom (ws)

Press open

Trim to ¼" (0.6 cm)

MAKE THE HANDLES

1 Cut the nylon webbing tape into two 7⅞" (20 cm) long pieces. Fold each piece in half widthwise and sew using 4" (10 cm) long seams along the center.

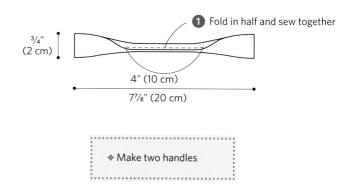

1 Fold in half and sew together

¾" (2 cm)

4" (10 cm)

7⅞" (20 cm)

✤ Make two handles

ATTACH THE HANDLES AND BINDING

1 Baste each handle to the lining.

2 With right sides together, sew the bias strip to the bag. Trim the batting and backing seam allowances to ¼" (0.6 cm). Wrap the bias strip around the seam allowances and slip-stitch to the lining (refer to page 73 for detailed binding instructions).

3 Fold the handles into the upright position and slip-stitch to the binding.

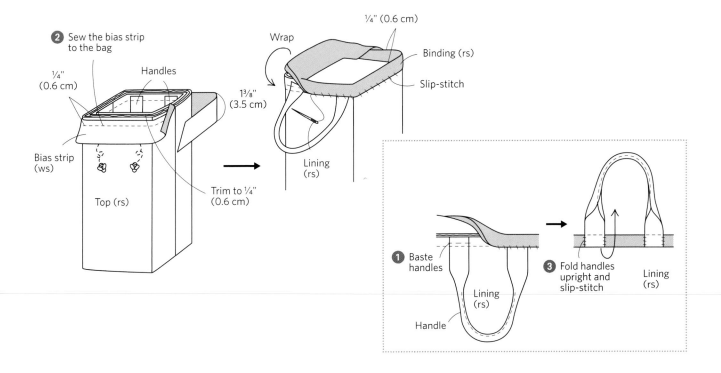

FINISH THE BAG

1 Topstitch ¹⁄₃₂" (0.1 cm) inside the gusset seams. Do not topstitch over the zigzag appliqué.

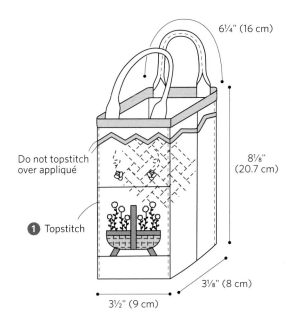

CONSTRUCTION STEPS

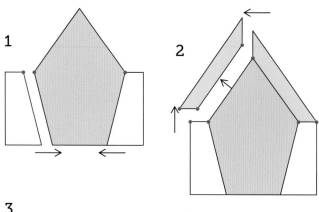

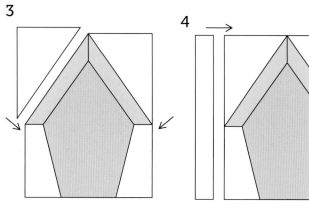

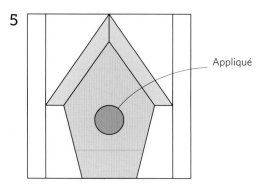

Appliqué

13 Birdhouse

This little birdhouse block is so easy to make, you can "build" it in just a few quick steps. For a natural look, I chose a wood grain print for the birdhouse and a twig print for the background, which makes the birdhouse appear as if it is hanging from a tree.

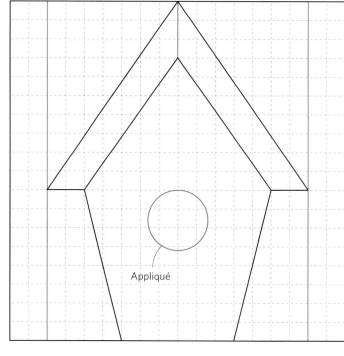

Appliqué

* When cutting your fabric, add ¼" (0.6 cm) seam allowance around each patchwork piece. Seam allowance is not pictured in the construction steps.
* When adjacent pieces are divided with a gray line, use the same fabric.
* Always press the seam allowance in the direction indicated by the arrows.
* The • marks to stop sewing at the seam allowance.

CONSTRUCTION STEPS

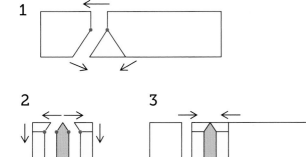

1

2   3

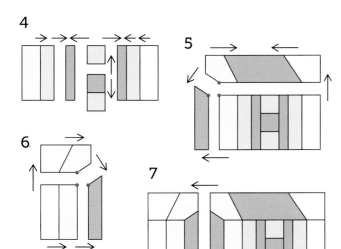

4

5

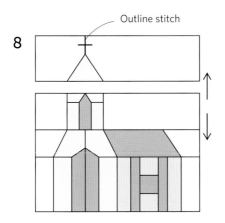

6

7

8

Outline stitch

- ❖ When cutting your fabric, add ¼" (0.6 cm) seam allowance around each patchwork piece. Seam allowance is not pictured in the construction steps.
- ❖ When adjacent pieces are divided with a gray line, use the same fabric.
- ❖ Always press the seam allowance in the direction indicated by the arrows.
- ❖ The • marks to stop sewing at the seam allowance.

14 Church

Create this picturesque church by sewing a patchwork steeple topped with an embroidered cross. I used a soft star print for the background fabric to give the impression of a peaceful night scene. This block is part of the Village Table Pocket project shown on page 36.

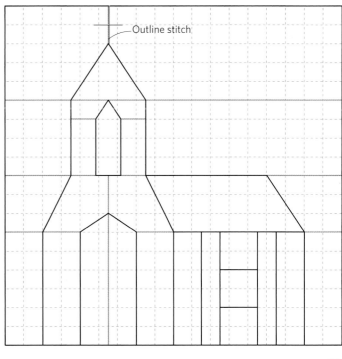

Outline stitch

15 Basic House

This basic house template is great on its own, but it can also be used as a foundation for constructing more elaborate abodes. Be your own architect by adding a chimney or changing the shape of the windows. This block is part of the Village Table Pocket project shown on page 36.

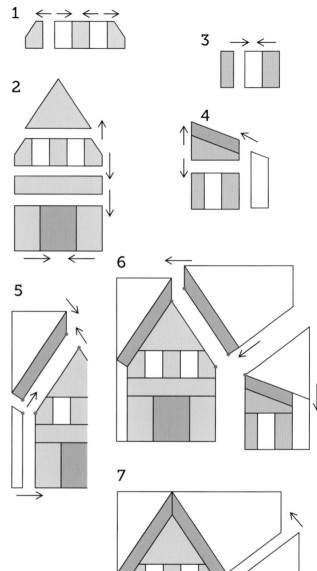

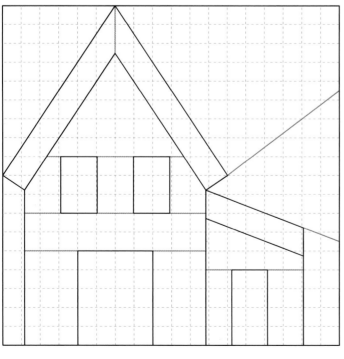

- ❖ When cutting your fabric, add ¼" (0.6 cm) seam allowance around each patchwork piece. Seam allowance is not pictured in the construction steps.
- ❖ When adjacent pieces are divided with a gray line, use the same fabric.
- ❖ Always press the seam allowance in the direction indicated by the arrows.
- ❖ The • marks to stop sewing at the seam allowance.

CONSTRUCTION STEPS

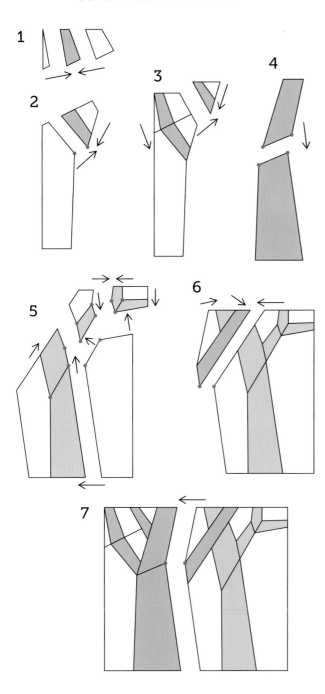

Get the look of a whole forest with just one simple block. Create life-like trees by arranging brown striped fabric vertically to replicate bark. Use a nature-inspired print for the background to add details such as vines and brambles. This block is part of the VillageTable Pocket project shown on page 36.

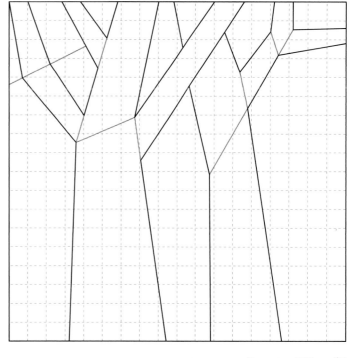

* When cutting your fabric, add ¼" (0.6 cm) seam allowance around each patchwork piece. Seam allowance is not pictured in the construction steps.
* When adjacent pieces are divided with a gray line, use the same fabric.
* Always press the seam allowance in the direction indicated by the arrows.
* The • marks to stop sewing at the seam allowance.

Village Table Pocket

Give your sewing tools a home of their own with this stunningly detailed pocket depicting a beautiful rural village. The Church, Basic House, and Forest blocks combine to create a picturesque scene set among a woodland of tree-printed background fabric.

Instructions on page 38

MATERIALS FOR VILLAGE TABLE POCKET

Patchwork fabric: Assorted scraps

Appliqué fabric: 1¾" × 15¾" (4.5 × 40 cm) dark brown print fabric

Top fabric: 9¾" × 43¼" (25 × 110 cm) tree print fabric

Backing fabric: 19¾" × 19¾" (50 × 50 cm)

Batting: 19¾" × 19¾" (50 × 50 cm)

Binding:

For outer edges:
One 1⅜" × 33½" (3.5 × 85 cm) beige print bias strip

One 1⅜" × 21¾" (3.5 × 55 cm) dark brown print bias strip

For pocket: One 1" × 17¾" (2.5 × 45 cm) bias strip

Embroidery floss: 6-strand embroidery floss in beige

LAYOUT DIAGRAM

FOUNDATION TOP

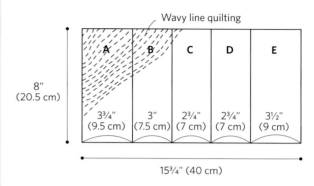

POCKET TOP

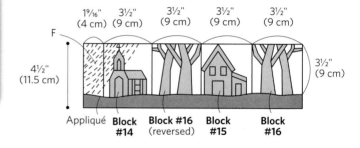

❖ Stitch in the ditch along all patchwork and appliqué pieces.

❖ Sew using ¼" (0.6 cm) seam allowance, unless otherwise noted.

❖ Finished Size: 8⅝" × 16⁵⁄₁₆" (21.9 × 41.4 cm)

CUTTING INSTRUCTIONS

Seam allowance is not included. Add ¼" (0.6 cm) seam allowance to all piece edges.

Trace and cut out the Block #14–#16 templates on pages 33–35. Using the templates, cut the patchwork pieces out of scrap fabric.

Cut out the following pieces, which do not have templates, according to the measurements below:

❖ **A:** 3¾" × 8" (9.5 × 20.5 cm) of top fabric
❖ **B:** 3" × 8" (7.5 × 20.5 cm) of top fabric
❖ **C:** 2¾" × 8" (7 × 20.5 cm) of top fabric
❖ **D:** 2¾" × 8" (7 × 20.5 cm) of top fabric
❖ **E:** 3½" × 8" (9 × 20.5 cm) of top fabric
❖ **F:** 1⁹⁄₁₆" × 4½" (4 × 11.5 cm) of top fabric

MAKE THE FOUNDATION TOP

① Sew pieces A–E together to make the foundation top.

② Cut the batting and backing slightly larger than the assembled foundation top. Layer the foundation top, batting, and backing. Quilt with wavy lines to create the appearance of wind.

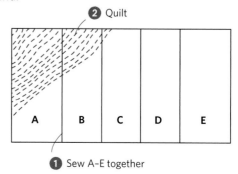

MAKE THE POCKET TOP

1 Follow the instructions on pages 33-35 to make Blocks #14-#16. Note: Make two of Block #16 (one using the template as it appears on page 35 and one with the template reversed). Embroider the cross on Block #14. Sew the blocks together and attach piece F to make the pocket top.

2 Use chalk to freehand a road on the appliqué fabric.

3 Cut along the chalk line leaving a ⅛" (0.3 cm) seam allowance.

4 Slip-stitch the appliqué road to the pocket top, tucking the seam allowance under with the needle tip as you work.

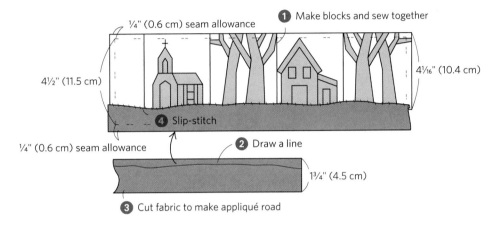

¼" (0.6 cm) seam allowance

1 Make blocks and sew together

4½" (11.5 cm)

4¹⁄₁₆" (10.4 cm)

4 Slip-stitch

¼" (0.6 cm) seam allowance

2 Draw a line

1¾" (4.5 cm)

3 Cut fabric to make appliqué road

ATTACH THE POCKET TOP AND FOUNDATION TOP

1 Cut the batting and backing slightly larger than the assembled pocket top. Layer the pocket top, batting, and backing. Quilt.

2 With right sides together, sew a bias strip to the upper edge of the pocket top. Trim the excess batting and backing seam allowances. Wrap the bias strip around the seam allowances and slip-stitch.

3 Layer the pocket top and foundation top. Baste together around the outer edges.

4 Draw the finishing line ¼" (0.6 cm) from the outer edges.

5 Sew the pocket divider seams, stitching through all layers.

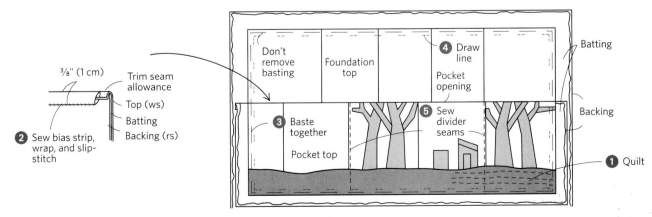

⅜" (1 cm)

Trim seam allowance

Top (ws)

Batting

Backing (rs)

2 Sew bias strip, wrap, and slip-stitch

Don't remove basting

Foundation top

4 Draw line

Pocket opening

Batting

3 Baste together

Pocket top

5 Sew divider seams

Backing

1 Quilt

SEW THE BINDING

1 Fold a short end of the beige bias strip back ¼" (0.6 cm) and press.

2 With right sides together, align the bias strip with the finishing line and backstitch.

3 At the corner, fold the bias strip at a 90° angle. Align the fold with the outer edge.

4 Insert the needle and draw it out along the next side.

5 Make one small backstitch, then continue sewing along the next side. This process will create a mitered corner.

6 Attach the dark brown print bias strip at the lower edge of the pocket top. To attach bias strips, overlap the ends ⅜" (1 cm). Trim the excess, then sew the overlapped ends together. Attach another beige bias strip, then continue sewing.

7 Refer to step 6 to attach the first and last bias strips.

8 Trim excess batting and backing seam allowances to ¼" (0.6 cm) along outer edges.

9 Wrap the bias strip around the seam allowance.

10 Slip-stitch the bias strip to the backing.

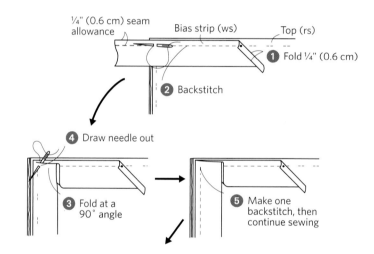

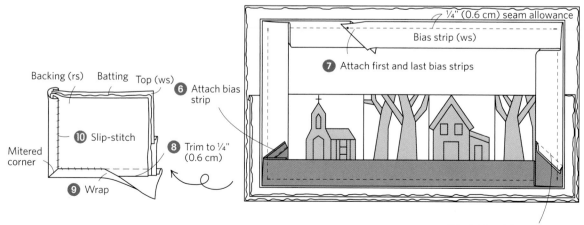

CONSTRUCTION STEPS

1

2

3

4

5

6

7

8

Appliqué

17 Village House

House motifs are popular among traditional quilt designs. Use an assortment of small prints to make the house's details, such as the porch and chimneys, stand out. I used a print of small buildings for the background, which creates the look of a village in the distance.

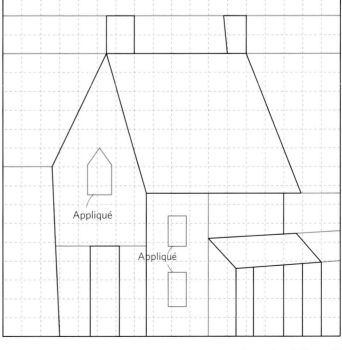

Appliqué

Appliqué

❖ When cutting your fabric, add ¼" (0.6 cm) seam allowance around each patchwork piece. Seam allowance is not pictured in the construction steps.

❖ When adjacent pieces are divided with a gray line, use the same fabric.

❖ Always press the seam allowance in the direction indicated by the arrows.

❖ The • marks to stop sewing at the seam allowance.

18 Fir Tree

This fir tree can be used for any quilt, but it is especially suited for holiday projects. Use a darker green for the bottom section of the tree to create a subtle gradation and add depth to your block. I also used a beige dot print for the background fabric to give the appearance of a snowstorm.

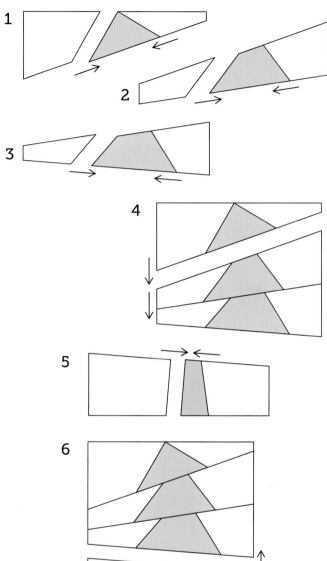

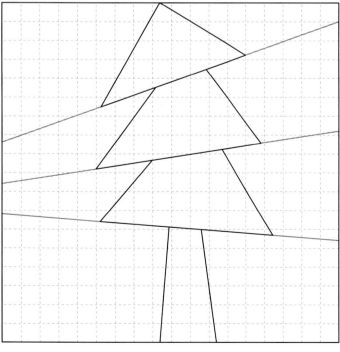

❖ When cutting your fabric, add ¼" (0.6 cm) seam allowance around each patchwork piece. Seam allowance is not pictured in the construction steps.

❖ When adjacent pieces are divided with a gray line, use the same fabric.

❖ Always press the seam allowance in the direction indicated by the arrows.

CONSTRUCTION STEPS

19 Basic Tree

This versatile tree block can be used for a variety of projects. Mix three different green prints for natural shading. Using a background fabric printed with leaves and branches makes the tree seem as if it's in the middle of a forest.

1

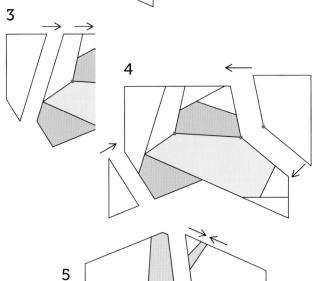

2

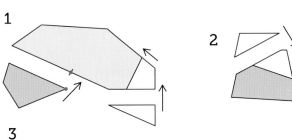

3

4

5

6

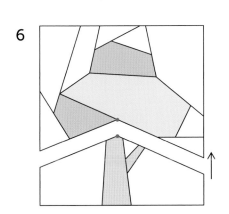

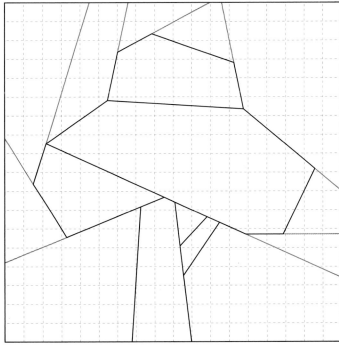

- When cutting your fabric, add ¼" (0.6 cm) seam allowance around each patchwork piece. Seam allowance is not pictured in the construction steps.
- When adjacent pieces are divided with a gray line, use the same fabric.
- Always press the seam allowance in the direction indicated by the arrows.
- The • marks to stop sewing at the seam allowance.

20 Pinwheel

This block was designed to look like a pinwheel blowing in the wind. I slightly angled the tip of the blades to suggest movement. The center is created with appliqué.

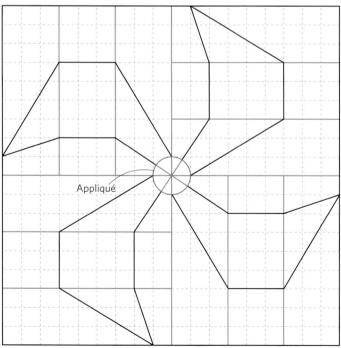

Appliqué

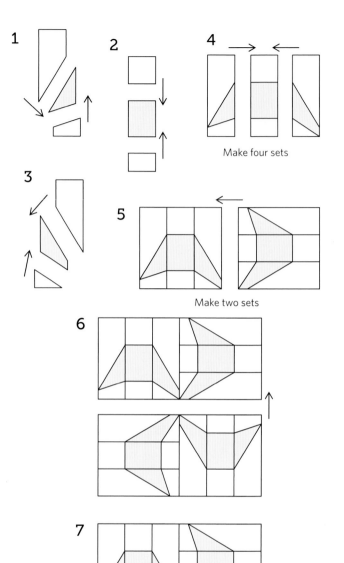

1

2

4

Make four sets

3

5

Make two sets

6

7

Appliqué

* When cutting your fabric, add ¼" (0.6 cm) seam allowance around each patchwork piece. Seam allowance is not pictured in the construction steps.
* When adjacent pieces are divided with a gray line, use the same fabric.
* Always press the seam allowance in the direction indicated by the arrows.

CONSTRUCTION STEPS

This block uses simple curves to create a quick and cheerful shamrock. I love the way the circular print of the background fabric mimics the curves of the patchwork and appliqué.

1

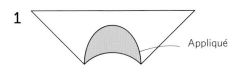

Appliqué

2

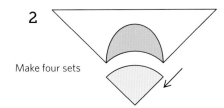

Make four sets

3

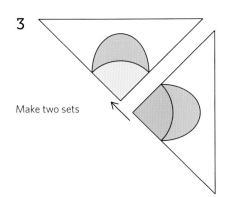

Make two sets

4

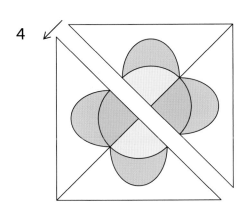

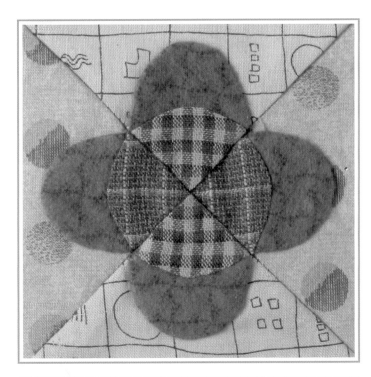

❖ When cutting your fabric, add ¼" (0.6 cm) seam allowance around each patchwork piece. Seam allowance is not pictured in the construction steps.

❖ Always press the seam allowance in the direction indicated by the arrows.

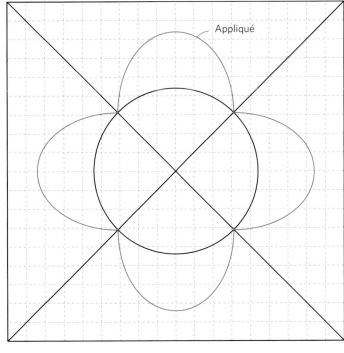

Appliqué

22 Cockscomb

The cockscomb flower is named for its resemblance to a rooster's crown. When designing this block, I used a compass to draw smoothly arcing lines. By using a darker color fabric for the curved sections of the block, you can create shadow, making the flower appear three-dimensional.

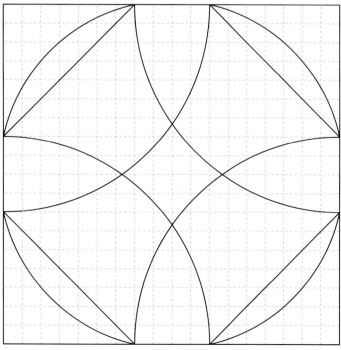

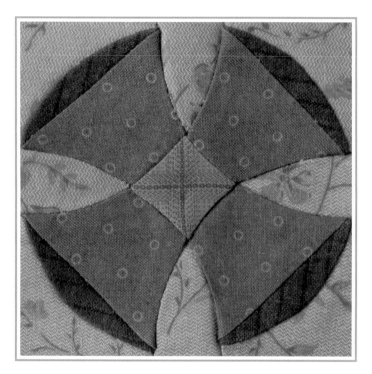

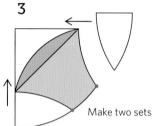

1 Mark

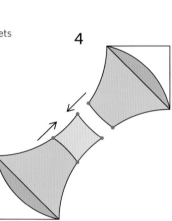

2

Make four sets

3

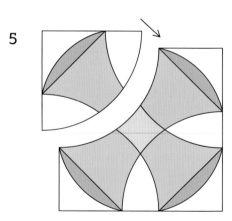

Make two sets

4

5

❖ When cutting your fabric, add ¼" (0.6 cm) seam allowance around each patchwork piece. Seam allowance is not pictured in the construction steps.

❖ Always press the seam allowance in the direction indicated by the arrows.

❖ The • marks to stop sewing at the seam allowance.

CONSTRUCTION STEPS

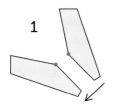

1

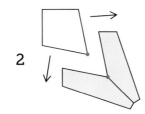

2

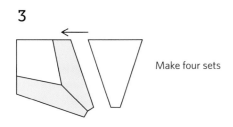

3

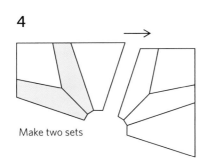

Make four sets

4

Make two sets

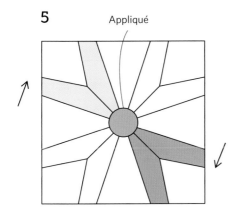

5

Appliqué

23 Primrose

Although the primrose is actually a wildflower, many gardeners cultivate this bloom for its beauty. I was inspired to create this simple and cute flower block using patchwork for the petals and appliqué for the center. When you play with fabric choice, as in the Primrose Shoulder Bag on page 48, these blocks will form a star pattern.

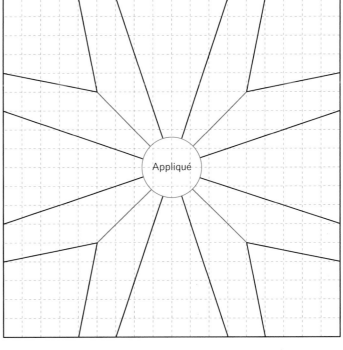

Appliqué

* When cutting your fabric, add ¼" (0.6 cm) seam allowance around each patchwork piece. Seam allowance is not pictured in the construction steps.
* When adjacent pieces are divided with a gray line, use the same fabric.
* Always press the seam allowance in the direction indicated by the arrows.
* The • marks to stop sewing at the seam allowance.

Primrose Shoulder Bag

Align Primrose blocks into rows of three to create a graphic star pattern. This versatile bag can be worn over the shoulder or across the body. With its thin and lightweight design, this bag is a great travel accessory.

MATERIALS FOR PRIMROSE SHOULDER BAG

Patchwork fabric: Assorted scraps

Main fabric: 13¾" × 27½" (35 × 70 cm) beige plaid fabric

Lining fabric: 15¾" × 27½" (40 × 70 cm)

Batting: 15¾" × 27½" (40 × 70 cm)

Fusible interfacing: Small scrap

Binding:

    For bag opening: One 1⅜" × 19¾" (3.5 × 50 cm) brown woven bias strip

    For seam allowances: One 1⅜" × 31½" (3.5 × 80 cm) brown woven bias strip

Magnetic snap: One ⅝" (1.5 cm) diameter metal snap

D-rings: Two ⅝" (1.5 cm) diameter metal D-rings

Strap: One ⅝" (1.5 cm) wide shoulder strap with metal swivel hooks

CUTTING INSTRUCTIONS

Seam allowance is not included. Add ¼" (0.6 cm) seam allowance to all piece edges.

Trace and cut out the Block #23 template on page 47. Using the template, cut the patchwork pieces out of scrap fabric. Cut out the following pieces, which do not have templates, according to the measurements below:

✤ **Tab (cut 2):** 1⅜" × 2" (3.5 × 5 cm) of scrap fabric

✤ **Tab backing (cut 2):** 1⅜" × 2" (3.5 × 5 cm) of scrap fabric

✤ **Tab interfacing (cut 2 without seam allowance):** 1⅜" × 2" (3.5 × 5 cm)

✤ **D-ring attachment (cut 2):** 1" × 1⁵⁄₁₆" (2.5 × 3.4 cm) of scrap fabric

✤ **D-ring attachment interfacing (cut 2 without seam allowance):** 1" × 1⁵⁄₁₆" (2.5 × 3.4 cm)

✤ **Back:** 8⅞" × 10⅞" (22.5 × 27.7 cm) of main fabric

LAYOUT DIAGRAM

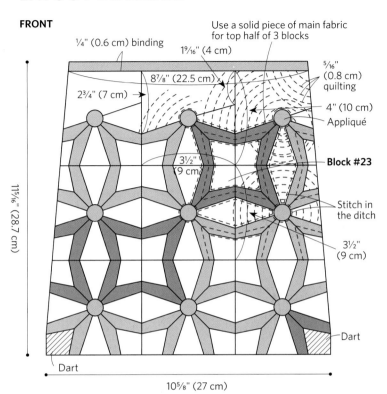

FRONT

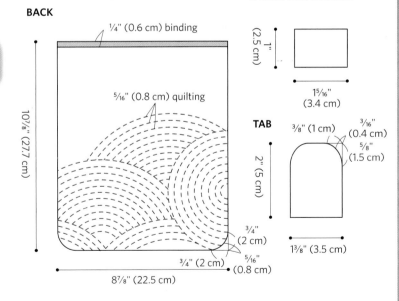

BACK

D-RING ATTACHMENT

TAB

✤ Stitch in the ditch along all patchwork and appliqué pieces.

✤ Sew using ¼" (0.6 cm) seam allowance, unless otherwise noted.

MAKE THE FRONT

1. Follow the instructions on page 47 to make nine of Block #23 (use a solid piece of main fabric for the top half of three blocks). To make the front, sew the blocks together in rows of three.

2. Cut the batting and lining slightly larger than the assembled front. Layer the front, batting, and front lining. Quilt, as shown in the layout diagram on page 49.

3. Make a template according to the dimensions in the layout diagram on page 49. Using the template, mark the finishing line, then trim.

4. Bind the top edge with the bias strip (refer to page 140 for detailed binding instructions).

5. Sew darts at the bottom corners. Slip-stitch the dart folds to the lining.

6. Sew around the outer edge with running stitch. Leave long thread tails. Pull the thread tails to gather the front into a rectangular shape.

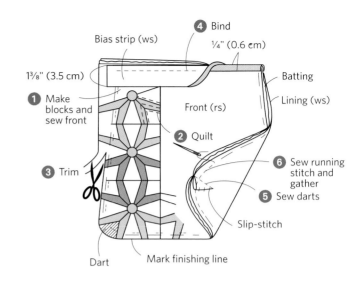

Bias strip (ws)

4 Bind
¼" (0.6 cm)

1⅜" (3.5 cm)

1 Make blocks and sew front

Front (rs)

Batting

Lining (ws)

2 Quilt

3 Trim

6 Sew running stitch and gather

5 Sew darts

Slip-stitch

Dart

Mark finishing line

MAKE THE BACK

1. Cut the batting and lining slightly larger than the back. Layer the back, batting, and back lining. Quilt with concentric circles about ⁵⁄₁₆" (0.8 cm) apart.

2. Bind the top edge with the bias strip (refer to page 140 for detailed binding instructions).

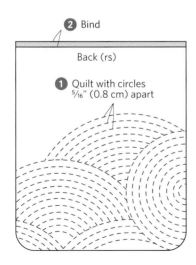

2 Bind

Back (rs)

1 Quilt with circles ⁵⁄₁₆" (0.8 cm) apart

MAKE THE TABS

1. Adhere fusible interfacing to the wrong side of each tab backing.

2. Layer each tab backing, tab top, and batting. Sew, leaving the bottoms open.

3. Trim the batting seam allowances. Turn right side out.

4. Slip-stitch the openings closed. Topstitch each tab with two rows of stitching ¼" (0.6 cm) apart. Attach a magnetic snap piece to each tab.

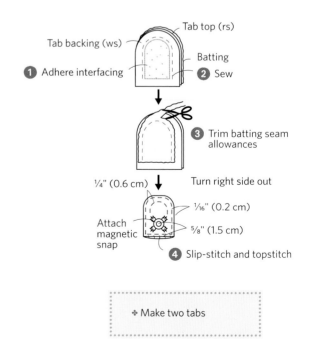

Tab backing (ws)

Tab top (rs)

Batting

1 Adhere interfacing

2 Sew

3 Trim batting seam allowances

¼" (0.6 cm)

Turn right side out

Attach magnetic snap

¹⁄₁₆" (0.2 cm)

⅝" (1.5 cm)

4 Slip-stitch and topstitch

✤ Make two tabs

MAKE THE D-RING ATTACHMENTS

1 Fold each D-ring attachment piece in half with right sides together and sew.

2 Center the seams and press. Adhere fusible interfacing. Turn right side out.

3 Slip-stitch the openings closed. Topstitch the long edges.

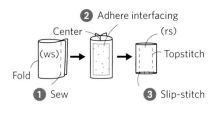

✤ Make two D-ring attachments

SEW THE BAG TOGETHER

1 Align the front and back with right sides facing out and sew together.

2 Bind the seam allowances with the bias strip (refer to page 92 for instructions on finishing seam allowances).

3 Slip-stitch the tabs to the lining.

4 Thread a metal D-ring onto each D-ring attachment.

5 Topstitch the D-ring attachments to the back.

6 Slip-stitch the D-ring attachments to the back.

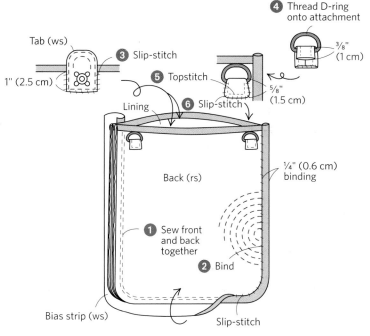

FINISH THE BAG

1 Clip a shoulder strap with metal swivel hooks onto the bag using the D-rings on the back.

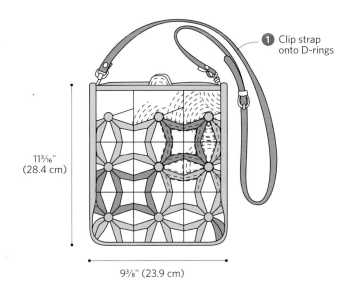

CONSTRUCTION STEPS

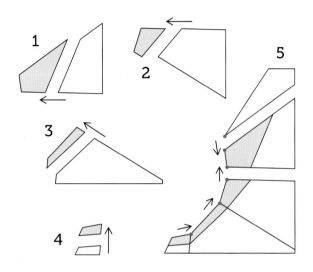

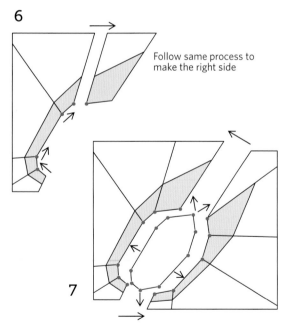

Follow same process to make the right side

24 Thread Clips

Make sure to preserve your angles to keep these thread clips looking sharp. Use a novelty print fabric for the background—the buttons and thread featured in this fabric make the thread clips seem like they are popping out of a sewing box.

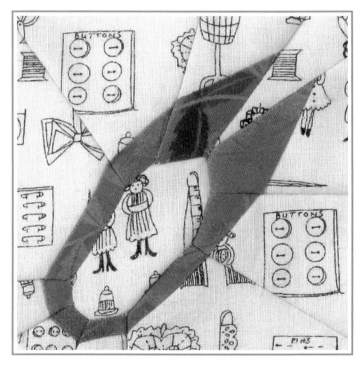

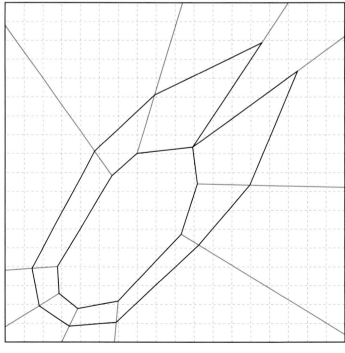

- When cutting your fabric, add ¼" (0.6 cm) seam allowance around each patchwork piece. Seam allowance is not pictured in the construction steps.
- When adjacent pieces are divided with a gray line, use the same fabric.
- Always press the seam allowance in the direction indicated by the arrows.
- The • marks to stop sewing at the seam allowance.

25 Scissors

Recreate your favorite sewing tools in fabric with these patchwork designs. Don't forget to draw the screw at the center of the blades to give your scissors a realistic look!

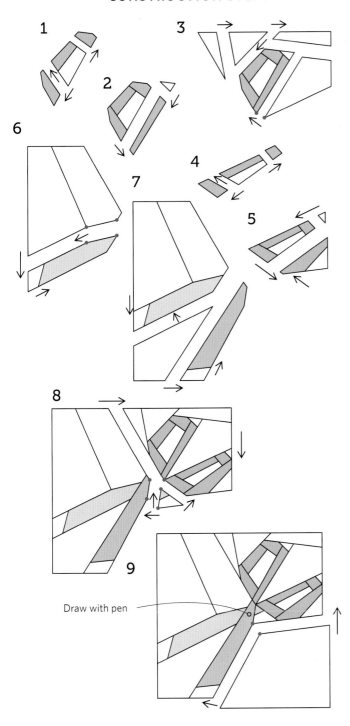

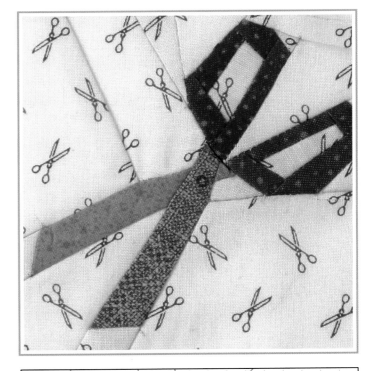

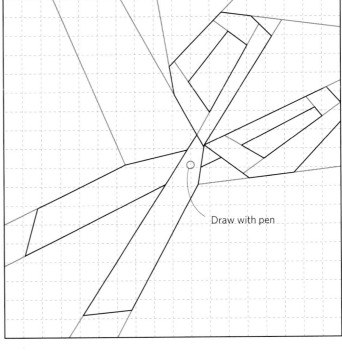

Draw with pen

- When cutting your fabric, add ¼" (0.6 cm) seam allowance around each patchwork piece. Seam allowance is not pictured in the construction steps.
- When adjacent pieces are divided with a gray line, use the same fabric.
- Always press the seam allowance in the direction indicated by the arrows.
- The • marks to stop sewing at the seam allowance.

26 Sewing Machine

This block was inspired by an antique treadle sewing machine rather than the state-of-the-art machines available today. I used black fabric to imitate the metal body and a wood grain print to recreate the base. A few simple embroidery stitches add special details like the needle and spool holder.

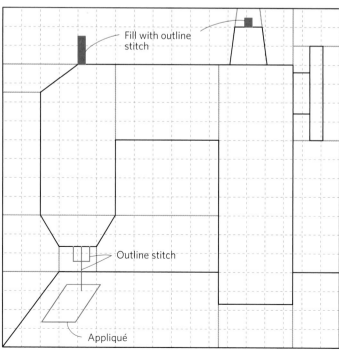

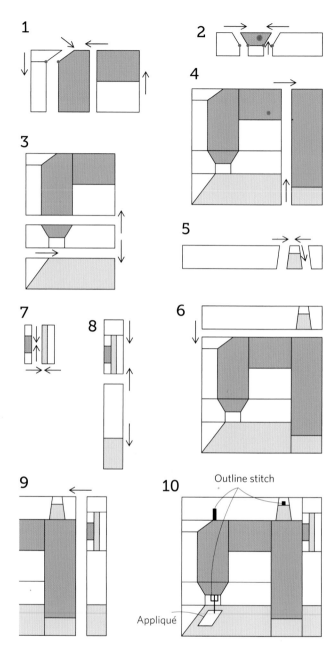

❖ When cutting your fabric, add ¼" (0.6 cm) seam allowance around each patchwork piece. Seam allowance is not pictured in the construction steps.

❖ When adjacent pieces are divided with a gray line, use the same fabric.

❖ Always press the seam allowance in the direction indicated by the arrows.

❖ The • marks to stop sewing at the seam allowance.

27 Spool #1

This block features a large, conical spool wound with lots of thread. No matter which spool design you choose, have fun experimenting with fabrics of different colors and patterns.

1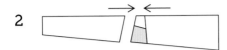

2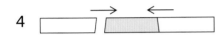

3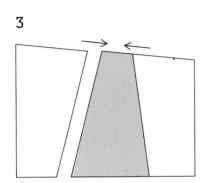

4

5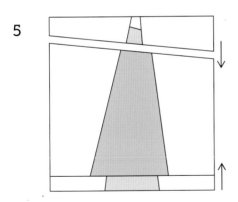

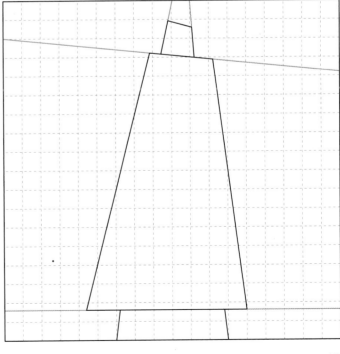

- When cutting your fabric, add ¼" (0.6 cm) seam allowance around each patchwork piece. Seam allowance is not pictured in the construction steps.
- When adjacent pieces are divided with a gray line, use the same fabric.
- Always press the seam allowance in the direction indicated by the arrows.

28 Spool #2

This spool has a simple, straight design. Since the shape of this spool is so classic, I chose a neutral color scheme. Use a striped fabric positioned horizontally to mimic the look of thread.

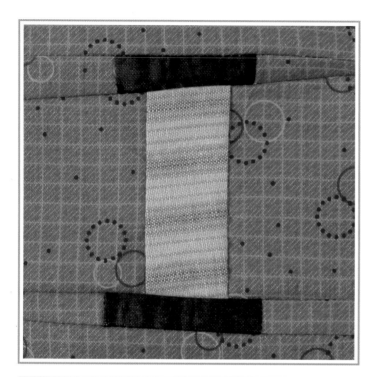

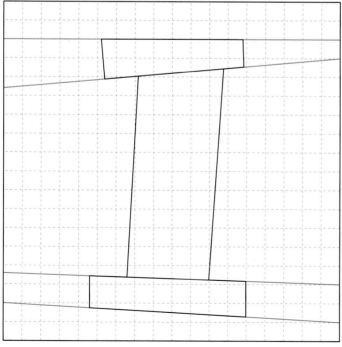

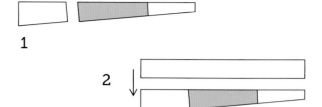

1

2

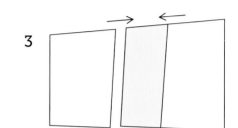

3

4

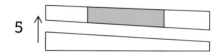

5

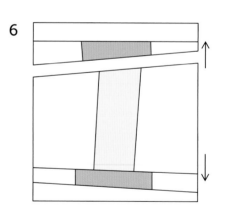

6

❖ When cutting your fabric, add ¼" (0.6 cm) seam allowance around each patchwork piece. Seam allowance is not pictured in the construction steps.

❖ When adjacent pieces are divided with a gray line, use the same fabric.

❖ Always press the seam allowance in the direction indicated by the arrows.

CONSTRUCTION STEPS

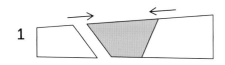

1

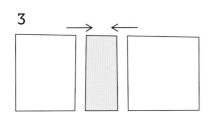

2

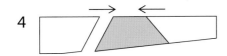

3

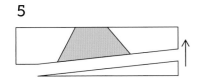

4

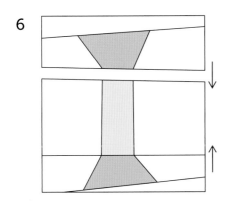

5

6

(29) # Spool #3

This block was inspired by a natural wooden spool. For the background, I found a fun abstract print that featured spool-shaped objects.

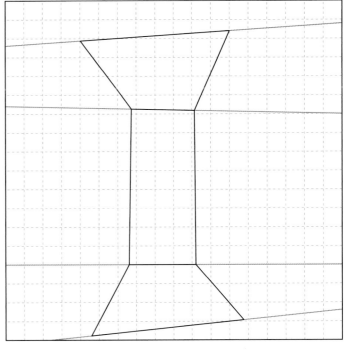

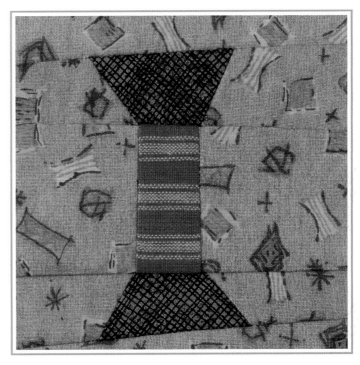

- ❖ When cutting your fabric, add ¼" (0.6 cm) seam allowance around each patchwork piece. Seam allowance is not pictured in the construction steps.
- ❖ When adjacent pieces are divided with a gray line, use the same fabric.
- ❖ Always press the seam allowance in the direction indicated by the arrows.

30 Winged Spool

The spool motif really stands out in this variation on a classic design. I used bold colors for some of the background pieces to suggest movement, almost making the spool appear as if it is flying! This block is used in the Winged Spool Purse project featured on the opposite page.

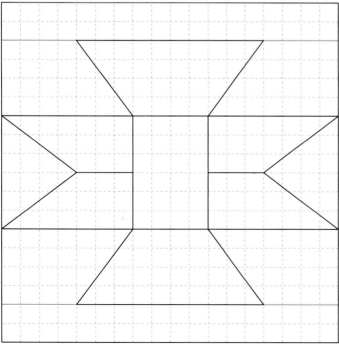

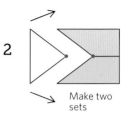
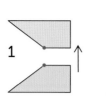
1

2

Make two sets

3

4

Make two sets

5

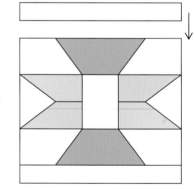

6

- ❖ When cutting your fabric, add ¼" (0.6 cm) seam allowance around each patchwork piece. Seam allowance is not pictured in the construction steps.
- ❖ When adjacent pieces are divided with a gray line, use the same fabric.
- ❖ Always press the seam allowance in the direction indicated by the arrows.
- ❖ The • marks to stop sewing at the seam allowance.

Winged Spool Purse

Let your quilting flag fly! Use the Winged Spool block to create this little purse with its unique rounded shape. The opening is rather small, so the front zipper offers convenience and easy access.

Instructions on page 60

MATERIALS FOR WINGED SPOOL PURSE

Patchwork fabric: Assorted scraps

Top gusset fabric: 9¾" × 9¾" (25 × 25 cm) beige checkered fabric

Bottom gusset fabric: 9¾" × 17¾" (25 × 45 cm) brown checkered fabric

Back fabric: 9¾" × 9¾" (25 × 25 cm) brown checkered fabric

Facing fabric: 4" × 7⅞" (10 × 20 cm)

Lining fabric: 19¾" × 31½" (50 × 80 cm)

Batting: 19¾" × 31½" (50 × 80 cm)

Binding: One 1" × 19¾" (2.5 × 50 cm) bias strip

Heavyweight fusible interfacing: 3⅛" × 27½" (8 × 70 cm)

Fusible interfacing: 4" × 7⅞" (10 × 20 cm)

Zipper: One 7" (18 cm) long zipper

Handle: One 8¼" (21 cm) wooden bead handle

Cord: 4" (10 cm) of 1/16" (0.2 cm) diameter cord

Zipper charm: One ⅝" × ¾" (1.5 × 2 cm) cylindrical wooden bead

LAYOUT DIAGRAM

GUSSET

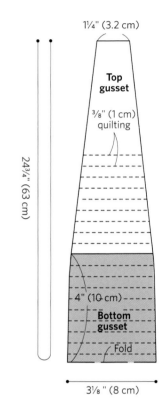

- Stitch in the ditch along all patchwork pieces.
- Sew using ¼" (0.6 cm) seam allowance, unless otherwise noted.

FACING

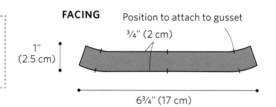

FRONT

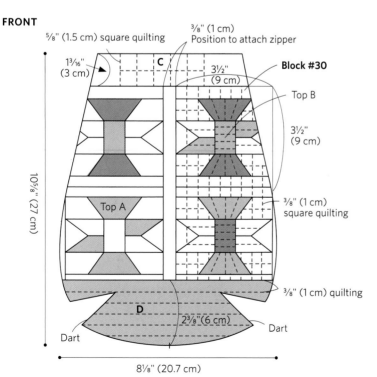

BACK

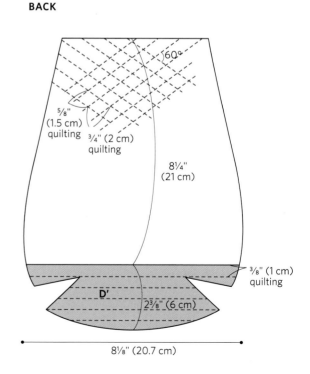

CUTTING INSTRUCTIONS

Seam allowance is not included. Add ¼" (0.6 cm) seam allowance to all piece edges.

Trace and cut out the templates on Pattern Sheet B and the Block #30 template on page 58. Cut out the pieces following the instructions listed on the templates.

MAKE THE FRONT

1. Follow the instructions on page 58 to make four of Block #30. Sew two blocks together vertically to make Top A. Repeat to make Top B.

2. Cut the batting and lining slightly larger than Top A. Layer Top A, batting, and lining. Baste. Stitch in the ditch and quilt with ⅜" (1 cm) squares. Repeat for Top B.

3. With right sides together, sew the zipper to Tops A and B. Trim the excess seam allowances and zipper, if necessary. Fold back the zipper seam allowance and slip-stitch to the lining.

4. Cut the batting and lining slightly larger than C. Layer C, batting, and lining. Baste, then quilt with ⅝" (1.5 cm) squares.

5. With right sides together, sew C to the top edge of the front.

6. Cut the batting and lining slightly larger than D. Layer D, batting, and lining. Baste, then quilt with horizontal lines about ⅜" (1 cm) apart.

7. With right sides together, sew D to the bottom edge of the front.

8. Using the template on Pattern Sheet B, trim the front into shape.

9. With right sides together, sew the bias strips to the seam allowances. Trim the excess seam allowances. Wrap the bias strips around the seam allowances and slip-stitch to the lining.

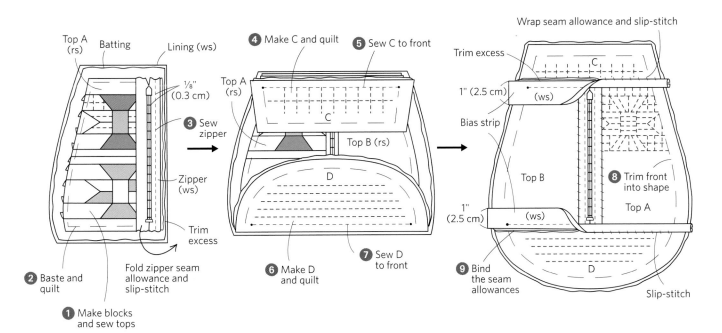

MAKE THE BACK

1 With right sides together, sew the back and D'.

2 Cut the batting and lining slightly larger than the assembled back. Layer the back, batting, and lining. Baste. Quilt the top with diagonal lines and the bottom with horizontal lines about ⅜" (1 cm) apart, as shown in the layout diagram on page 60.

3 Sew the darts at the bottom corners. Slip-stitch the seam allowances to the lining. Repeat to sew the darts on the front, making sure to press and sew the dart folds in the opposite direction from the back.

2 Quilt back

Lining (rs)

Slip-stitch

Baste

1 Sew back and D'

3 Sew darts

MAKE THE GUSSET

1 With right sides together, sew the top gussets to the bottom gusset.

2 Cut the batting and lining slightly larger than the assembled gusset. Cut the heavyweight fusible interfacing the size of the assembled gusset but without seam allowance. Adhere the heavyweight fusible interfacing to the wrong side of the gusset lining.

3 Layer the gusset, batting, and lining. Baste, then quilt with horizontal lines about ⅜" (1 cm) apart.

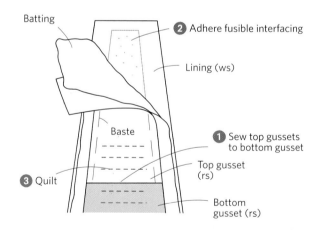

Batting

2 Adhere fusible interfacing

Lining (ws)

Baste

1 Sew top gussets to bottom gusset

Top gusset (rs)

3 Quilt

Bottom gusset (rs)

SEW THE BAG TOGETHER

1 With right sides together, sew the gusset to the front and back.

2 Trim all seam allowances, except the gusset lining seam allowances, to ¼" (0.6 cm). Do not trim the gusset lining seam allowances.

3 Wrap the gusset lining seam allowances around the trimmed seam allowances and slip-stitch to the lining.

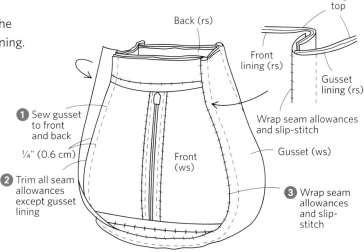

MAKE THE FACING

1 Cut the fusible interfacing the size of the facing but without seam allowance. Adhere the fusible interfacing to the wrong side of the facing.

2 Sew the facing together along the short edges.

3 With right sides together, sew the facing to the bag opening, leaving two ¾" (2 cm) openings at the positions to attach the handle. Trim the excess seam allowances.

4 Fold the facing to the inside of the bag. Press. Slip-stitch the facing to the lining.

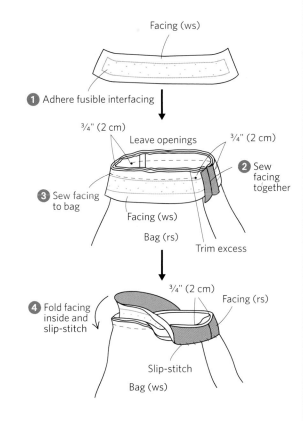

ATTACH THE HANDLE

1. Insert the metal ends of the handle into the openings.

2. Slip-stitch the openings closed.

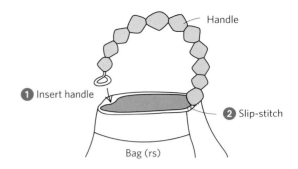

Handle

1 Insert handle

2 Slip-stitch

Bag (rs)

ATTACH THE ZIPPER CHARMS TO FINISH THE BAG

1. Fold the cord in half. Thread the loop through the zipper pull, then pass the ends of the cord through the loop.

2. Thread the bead onto the cord and tie a knot.

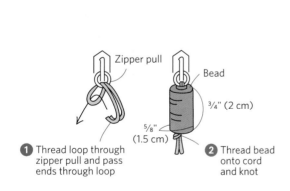

Zipper pull

Bead

¾" (2 cm)

⅝" (1.5 cm)

1 Thread loop through zipper pull and pass ends through loop

2 Thread bead onto cord and knot

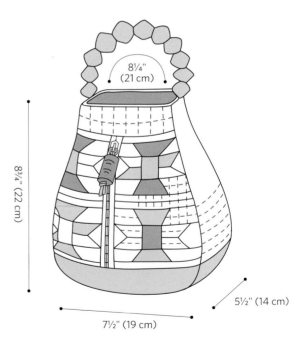

8¼" (21 cm)

8¾" (22 cm)

5½" (14 cm)

7½" (19 cm)

CONSTRUCTION STEPS

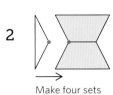

1

2

Make four sets

3

4

Make two sets

5

6

31 Small Spools

This hardworking little block does double duty. Position it upright, as featured below, for a frame-shaped block with a small spool in each corner. Rotate it 90° and you have a block with bows. This block is used in the Spool Sewing Box project on page 66.

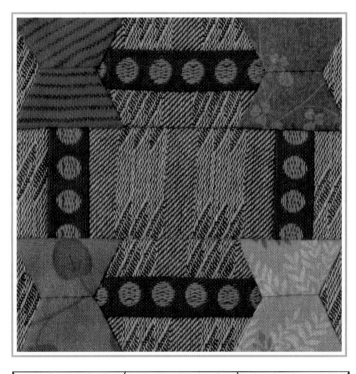

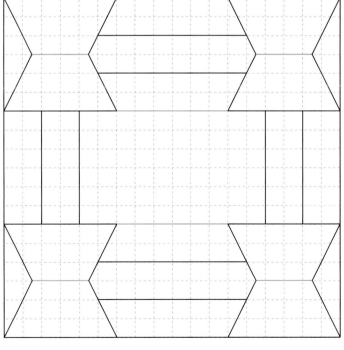

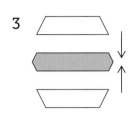

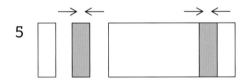

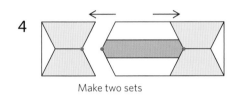

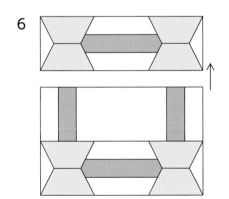

- ❖ When cutting your fabric, add ¼" (0.6 cm) seam allowance around each patchwork piece. Seam allowance is not pictured in the construction steps.
- ❖ When adjacent pieces are divided with a gray line, use the same fabric.
- ❖ Always press the seam allowance in the direction indicated by the arrows.
- ❖ The • marks to stop sewing at the seam allowance.

Spool Sewing Box

This spool-inspired box is the perfect caddy for all your sewing essentials. With a sturdy, suitcase-shaped design and large inside pockets, this box is great for transporting your tools to class or keeping your sewing room organized.

Instructions on page 68

MATERIALS FOR SPOOL SEWING BOX

Patchwork fabric: Assorted scraps

Front/bottom fabric: 11¾" × 11¾" (30 × 30 cm) beige woven fabric

Back fabric: 6" × 11¾" (15 × 30 cm) gray woven fabric

Gusset fabric: 7⅞" × 21¾" (20 × 55 cm) black and white polka dot fabric

Handle fabric: 2" × 6" (5 × 15 cm) dark green corduroy fabric

Lining/pocket fabric: 17¾" × 23⅝" (45 × 60 cm)

Batting: 17¾" × 23⅝" (45 × 60 cm)

Binding:

    For pocket: One 1⅜" × 9¾" (3.5 × 25 cm) red striped bias strip

    For seam allowances: One 1⅜" × 47¼" (3.5 × 120 cm) dark brown plaid bias strip

Fusible interfacing: 9¾" × 19¾" (25 × 50 cm)

Zipper: One 18" (45.5 cm) long zipper

Zipper charms: Two wooden zipper charms

Cord: 7⅞" (20 cm) of 1/32" (0.1 cm) diameter cord

CUTTING INSTRUCTIONS

Seam allowance is not included. Add ¼" (0.6 cm) seam allowance to all piece edges.

Trace and cut out the Block #31 template on page 65. Using the template, cut the patchwork pieces out of scrap fabric.

Cut out the following pieces, which do not have templates, according to the measurements below:

❖ **Border strip A (cut 3):** ⅝" × 3½" (1.5 × 9 cm) of front/bottom fabric

❖ **Border strip B:** ⅝" × 8⅞" (1.5 × 22.5 cm) of front/bottom fabric

❖ **Bottom:** 2¾" × 8⅞" (7 × 22.5 cm) of front/bottom fabric

❖ **Back:** 4¾" × 8⅞" (12 × 22.5 cm) of back fabric

❖ **Pocket:** 6" × 8⅞" (15 × 22.5 cm) of lining/pocket fabric

❖ **Pocket interfacing (cut without seam allowance):** 6" × 8⅞" (15 × 22.5 cm)

❖ **Gusset:** 1¾" × 17¾" (4.5 × 45 cm) of gusset fabric

❖ **Gusset lining :** 1¾" × 17¾" (4.5 × 45 cm) of lining/pocket fabric

❖ **Gusset interfacing (cut without seam allowance):** 1¾" × 17¾" (4.5 × 45 cm)

❖ **Handle (cut on the bias):** ⅞" × 5⅛" (2.3 × 13 cm) of handle fabric

❖ **Handle lining (cut on the bias):** ⅞" × 5⅛" (2.3 × 13 cm) of handle fabric

❖ **Handle interfacing (cut without seam allowance):** ⅞" × 5⅛" (2.3 × 13 cm)

LAYOUT DIAGRAM

BOX TOP

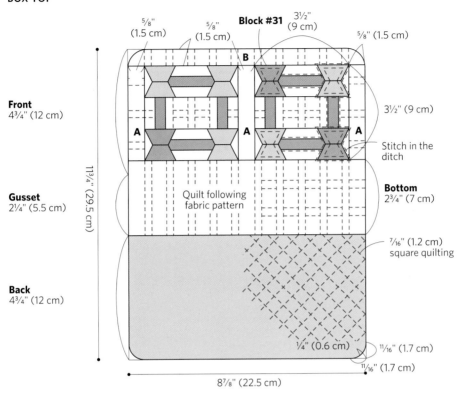

⁵⁄₈" (1.5 cm)
⁵⁄₈" (1.5 cm)
Block #31
3½" (9 cm)
⁵⁄₈" (1.5 cm)

B

Front
4¾" (12 cm)

A   A   A

3½" (9 cm)

Stitch in the ditch

11¾" (29.5 cm)

Gusset
2¼" (5.5 cm)

Quilt following fabric pattern

Bottom
2¾" (7 cm)

⁷⁄₁₆" (1.2 cm) square quilting

Back
4¾" (12 cm)

¼" (0.6 cm)
11⁄₁₆" (1.7 cm)
11⁄₁₆" (1.7 cm)

8⅞" (22.5 cm)

GUSSET

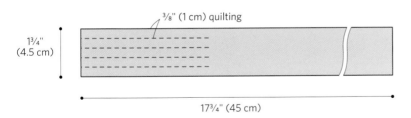

⅜" (1 cm) quilting

1¾" (4.5 cm)

17¾" (45 cm)

✤ Stitch in the ditch along all patchwork pieces.

✤ Sew using ¼" (0.6 cm) seam allowance, unless otherwise noted.

POCKET

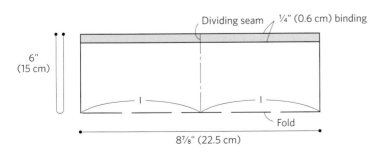

Dividing seam
¼" (0.6 cm) binding

6" (15 cm)

Fold

8⅞" (22.5 cm)

HANDLE (cut on the bias)

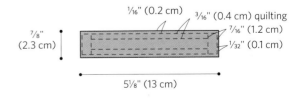

1⁄₁₆" (0.2 cm)
³⁄₁₆" (0.4 cm) quilting
⁷⁄₁₆" (1.2 cm)
1⁄₃₂" (0.1 cm)

⅞" (2.3 cm)

5⅛" (13 cm)

MAKE THE BOX TOP

1. Follow the instructions on page 65 to make two of Block #31.

2. To make the front, sew the three A border strips and the blocks together, then attach the B border strip at the top.

3. To make the box top, sew the bottom and back to the front.

4. Cut the lining and batting slightly larger than the assembled box top. Layer the box top, batting, and lining. Baste. Quilt, as shown in the layout diagram on page 69.

5. Trim the corners into a rounded shape.

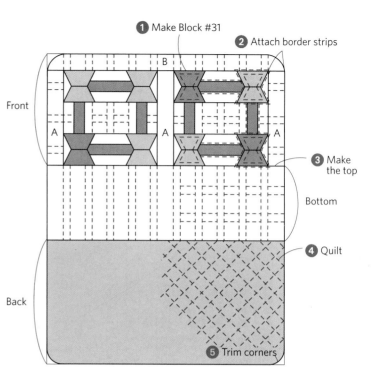

MAKE THE POCKET

1. Adhere the fusible interfacing to the wrong side of the pocket.

2. Fold the pocket in half.

3. Bind the long edge of the pocket with the bias strip (refer to page 140 for binding instructions).

4. Baste the pocket to the lining.

5. Slip-stitch the folded edge of the pocket to the lining. Make sure the stitching is not visible from the outside of the box.

6. Sew to divide the pocket into two sections.

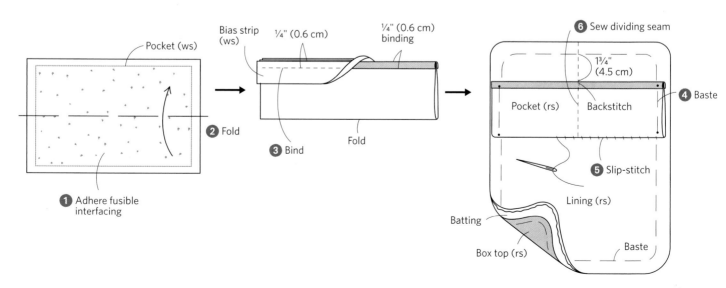

MAKE THE GUSSET

1. Adhere the fusible interfacing to the wrong side of the gusset lining.

2. With right sides together, baste the zipper to one side of the gusset. Trim excess zipper length, if necessary.

3. With right sides together, layer the gusset lining, gusset, and batting. Sew together along one long side. Fold gusset lining to inside and press.

4. Topstitch the gusset along the zipper.

5. Baste the layers together along three sides. Quilt with horizontal lines about ⅜" (1 cm) apart.

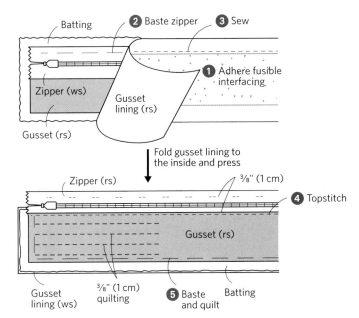

Batting 2 Baste zipper 3 Sew
Zipper (ws) 1 Adhere fusible interfacing
Gusset lining (rs)
Gusset (rs)

Fold gusset lining to the inside and press

Zipper (rs) ⅜" (1 cm) 4 Topstitch
Gusset (rs)
Gusset lining (ws) ⅜" (1 cm) quilting 5 Baste and quilt Batting

MAKE THE HANDLE

1. Adhere the fusible interfacing to the wrong side of the handle lining.

2. With right sides together, layer the handle lining, handle, and batting. Sew along three sides, leaving one short side open. Turn right side out.

3. Slip-stitch the opening closed

4. Quilt, as shown in the layout diagram on page 69.

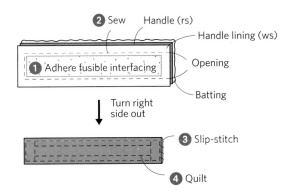

2 Sew Handle (rs)
Handle lining (ws)
1 Adhere fusible interfacing Opening
Batting

Turn right side out

3 Slip-stitch
4 Quilt

SEW THE HANDLE TO THE GUSSET

1 Align the center of the handle with the center of the gusset. Topstitch the handle to the gusset along the short ends

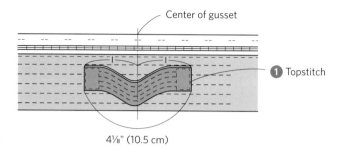

Center of gusset

1 Topstitch

4⅛" (10.5 cm)

SEW THE GUSSET TO THE BOX

1 Align the wrong side of the gusset with the right side of the box lining along the front. Sew the zipper to the box lining.

2 Align the wrong side of the gusset with the right side of the box lining along the back. Baste.

3 Sew the gusset and box together.

4 Trim the excess seam allowances and zipper, if necessary.

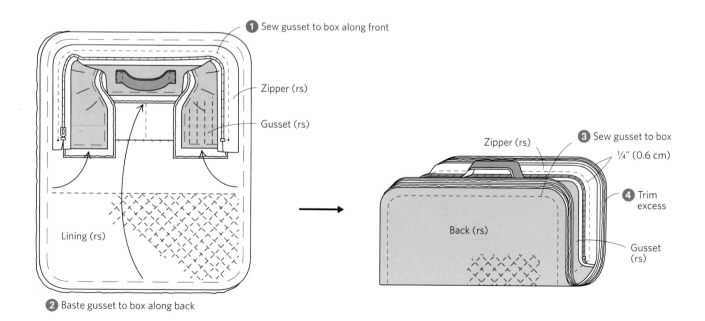

1 Sew gusset to box along front

Zipper (rs)

Gusset (rs)

Lining (rs)

2 Baste gusset to box along back

Zipper (rs)

3 Sew gusset to box

¼" (0.6 cm)

4 Trim excess

Back (rs)

Gusset (rs)

FINISH THE SEAM ALLOWANCES

1 Sew the bias strip to the seam allowance. Fold the short ends of the bias strip and overlap to finish.

2 Wrap the bias strip around the seam allowance and slip-stitch.

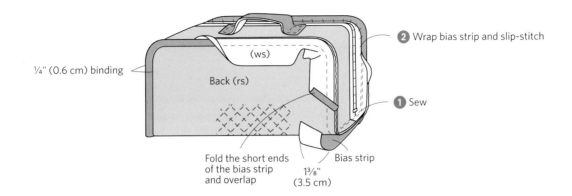

2 Wrap bias strip and slip-stitch

¼" (0.6 cm) binding

(ws)

Back (rs)

1 Sew

Fold the short ends of the bias strip and overlap

Bias strip

1⅜" (3.5 cm)

ATTACH THE ZIPPER CHARMS AND FINISH THE BOX

1 Thread one zipper charm onto the cord. Thread the cord through the zipper pull and knot.

2 Thread the other zipper charm onto the cord and knot.

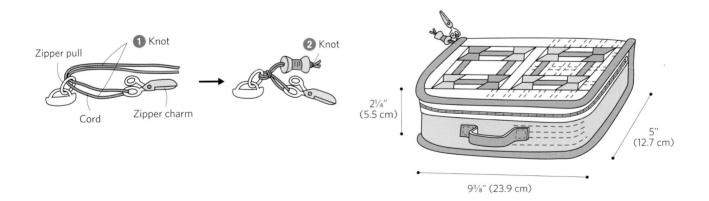

Zipper pull

1 Knot

2 Knot

Cord

Zipper charm

2¼" (5.5 cm)

9⅜" (23.9 cm)

5" (12.7 cm)

32 Cat

This block features the silhouette of a graceful cat. I used a combination of black prints for my block, but feel free to mix different patterns and colors to recreate your favorite feline. This block is part of the Cat & Dog Box project shown on page 76.

CONSTRUCTION STEPS

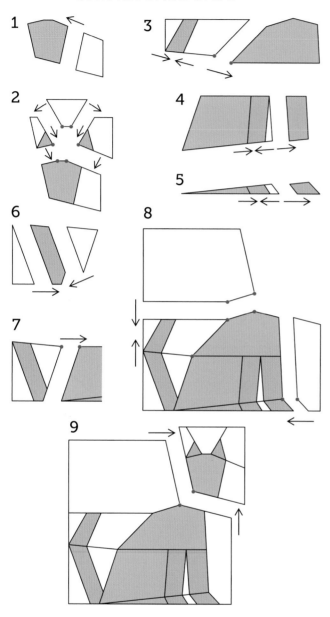

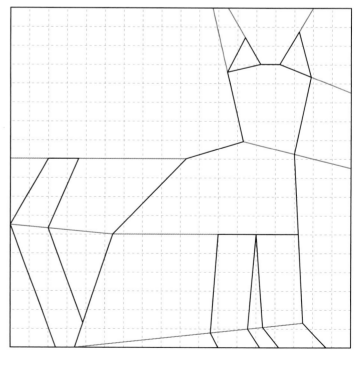

- When cutting your fabric, add ¼" (0.6 cm) seam allowance around each patchwork piece. Seam allowance is not pictured in the construction steps.
- When adjacent pieces are divided with a gray line, use the same fabric.
- Always press the seam allowance in the direction indicated by the arrows.
- The • marks to stop sewing at the seam allowance.

CONSTRUCTION STEPS

33 Dog

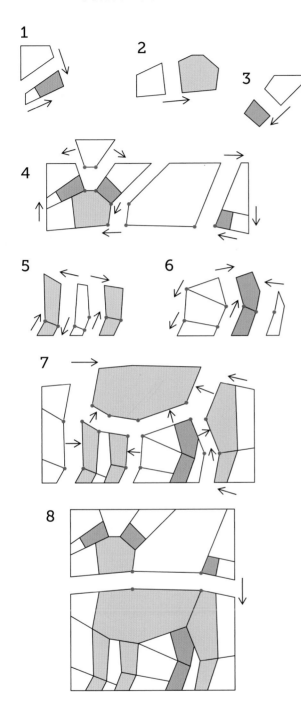

My dog Linus served as the model for this block. I used a darker material for one of his back legs to create shadow and depth. This block is part of the Cat & Dog Box project shown on page 76.

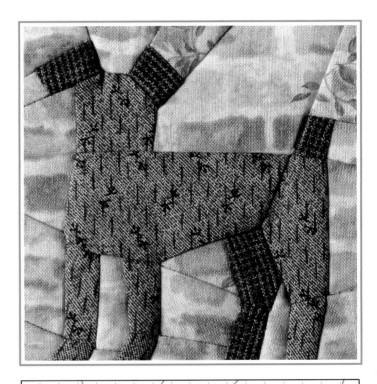

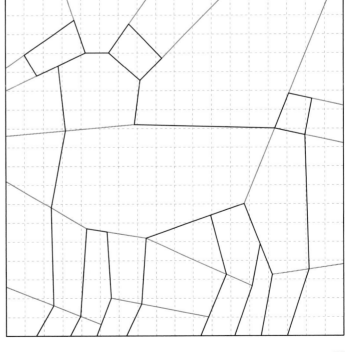

- When cutting your fabric, add ¼" (0.6 cm) seam allowance around each patchwork piece. Seam allowance is not pictured in the construction steps.
- When adjacent pieces are divided with a gray line, use the same fabric.
- Always press the seam allowance in the direction indicated by the arrows.
- The • marks to stop sewing at the seam allowance.

Cat & Dog Box

Create this little box for odds and ends, or use it as a home for your pet's favorite toys and treats. Use the Cat and Dog blocks for the flap and the Diamond in a Box block (see page 143) for the sides. Don't forget to choose a fun lining fabric that complements the outside of the box.

Instructions on page 78

MATERIALS FOR CAT & DOG BOX

Patchwork fabric: Assorted scraps

Bottom fabric: 6" × 9¾" (15 × 25 cm) dark brown fabric

Backing fabric: 17¾" × 21¾" (45 × 55 cm)

Batting: 17¾" × 21¾" (45 × 55 cm)

Lining fabric: 17¾" × 21¾" (45 × 55 cm)

Binding: One 1⅜" × 23⅝" (3.5 × 60 cm) green flannel bias strip

Cord: 2⅜" (6 cm) of ⅛" (0.3 cm) diameter green cord

Button: One ⅝" (1.4 cm) diameter button

Cardboard: 11¾" × 16½" (29.7 × 42 cm) cardboard

CUTTING INSTRUCTIONS

Seam allowance is not included. Add ¼" (0.6 cm) seam allowance to all piece edges.

Trace and cut out the Block #32, #33, and #78 templates on pages 74, 75, and 143. Using the templates, cut the patchwork pieces out of scrap fabric.

Cut out the following pieces, which do not have templates, according to the measurements below:

❖ **Flap lining:** About 4¹⁄₁₆" × 7¾" (10.4 × 19.4 cm) of lining fabric

❖ **Bottom:** 3½" × 7" (9 × 18 cm) of bottom fabric

LAYOUT DIAGRAM

FLAP

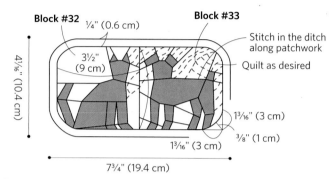

Block #32 — ¼" (0.6 cm) — Block #33
Stitch in the ditch along patchwork
Quilt as desired
3½" (9 cm)
4¹⁄₁₆" (10.4 cm)
1³⁄₁₆" (3 cm)
⅜" (1 cm)
1³⁄₁₆" (3 cm)
7¾" (19.4 cm)

BOX

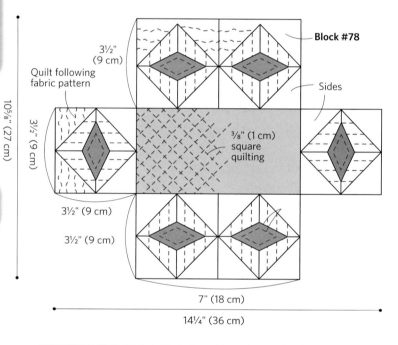

Block #78
3½" (9 cm)
Quilt following fabric pattern
Sides
⅜" (1 cm) square quilting
10⅝" (27 cm)
3½" (9 cm)
3½" (9 cm)
3½" (9 cm)
7" (18 cm)
14¼" (36 cm)

❖ Stitch in the ditch along all patchwork pieces.
❖ Sew using ¼" (0.6 cm) seam allowance, unless otherwise noted.

MAKE THE FLAP

1. Follow the instructions on pages 74 and 75 to make Blocks #32 and #33. Sew the two blocks together to make the flap top.

2. Cut the batting and backing slightly larger than the assembled flap top. Layer the flap top, batting, and backing. Baste. Stitch in the ditch along all patchwork pieces, then quilt remaining areas as desired.

3. Draw the finishing line ¼" (0.6 cm) from the outer edges. Trace the finishing line to make a template of the top. Using the template, cut a piece of cardboard into the shape of the flap top.

4. Trim the batting and backing into a rounded shape that is just slightly larger than the flap top.

5. Layer the flap lining, cardboard, and flap top. Baste.

6. Fold the cord in half and baste to the flap lining.

7. Bind the flap using the bias strip (refer to page 73 for detailed binding instructions).

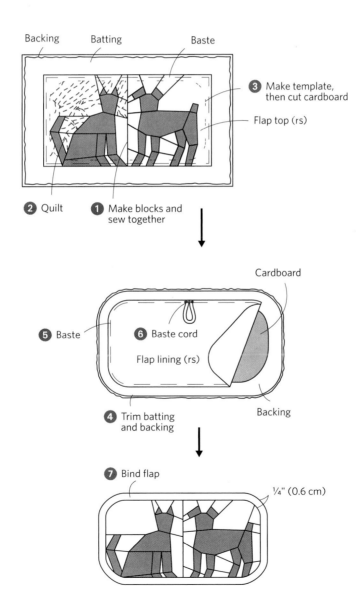

MAKE THE BOX

1 Follow the instructions on page 143 to make six of Block #78. Sew two blocks together to make one long side. Repeat to make the other long side.

2 To make the box top, sew the sides and bottom together, starting and stopping at the seam allowances.

3 Cut the batting and backing slightly larger than the assembled box top. Layer the box top, batting, and backing. Baste.

4 Stitch in the ditch along all patchwork pieces. Quilt the bottom with ⅜" (1 cm) squares and quilt remaining areas following the fabric pattern.

5 Align box top and lining with right sides together. Sew together along four corners, starting and stopping at the seam allowances. Make clips into the seam allowance at the corners.

6 Trim the batting and backing seam allowances to ¼" (0.6 cm). Turn right side out.

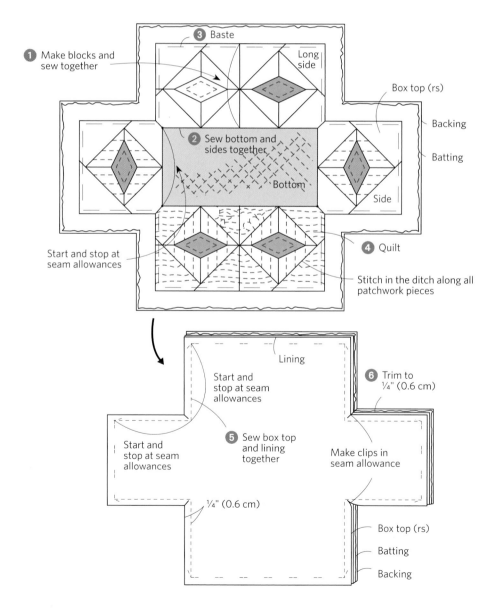

3 Baste

1 Make blocks and sew together

Long side

Box top (rs)

Backing

Batting

2 Sew bottom and sides together

Bottom

Side

Start and stop at seam allowances

4 Quilt

Stitch in the ditch along all patchwork pieces

Lining

Start and stop at seam allowances

6 Trim to ¼" (0.6 cm)

Start and stop at seam allowances

5 Sew box top and lining together

Make clips in seam allowance

¼" (0.6 cm)

Box top (rs)

Batting

Backing

MAKE THE BOX (continued)

7 On the right side, topstitch the bottom along three sides.

8 Cut pieces of cardboard into the shape of the bottom and each side.

9 Insert the cardboard into the bottom.

10 Topstitch the bottom closed along the remaining side.

11 Insert the cardboard into each side.

12 Fold in the seam allowances and slip-stitch each side closed.

13 Fold the sides into the upright position and whipstitch together.

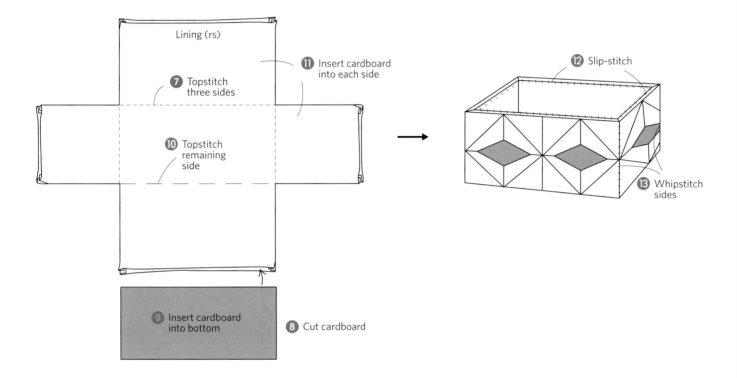

FINISH THE BOX

1 Whipstitch the flap to the box along one side.

2 Attach a button to the front of the box.

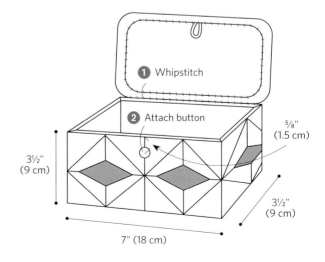

34 Scaredy Cat

I find it amazing that a few little stitches can capture an animal's facial expression so accurately. Outline stitch with embroidery floss to create this cat's wispy whiskers and worried mouth.

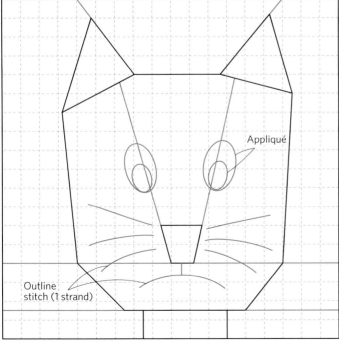

Appliqué

Outline stitch (1 strand)

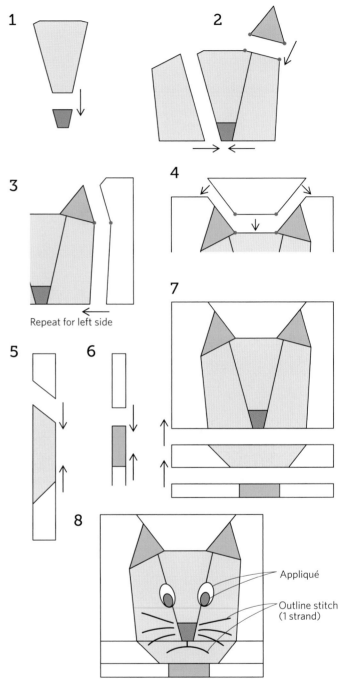

1

2

3

Repeat for left side

4

5

6

7

8

Appliqué

Outline stitch (1 strand)

* When cutting your fabric, add ¼" (0.6 cm) seam allowance around each patchwork piece. Seam allowance is not pictured in the construction steps.
* When adjacent pieces are divided with a gray line, use the same fabric.
* Always press the seam allowance in the direction indicated by the arrows.
* The • marks to stop sewing at the seam allowance.

CONSTRUCTION STEPS

This happy-go-lucky dog is ready to play! I pieced this block onto a fun background print so it looks like this canine is about to go fetch.

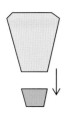
1

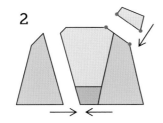
2

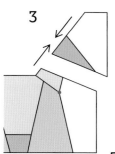
3

Repeat for left side

4
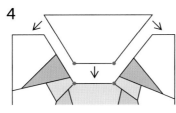

5
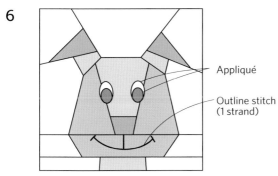

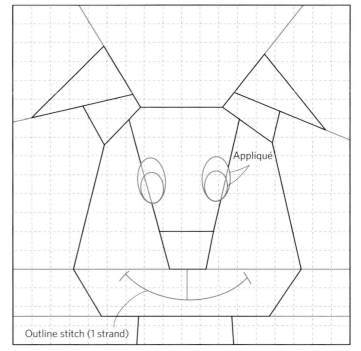

6
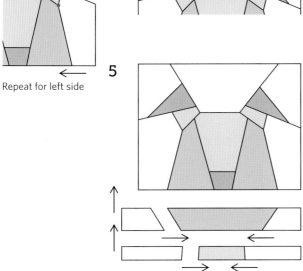

Appliqué

Outline stitch
(1 strand)

Appliqué

Outline stitch (1 strand)

- When cutting your fabric, add ¼" (0.6 cm) seam allowance around each patchwork piece. Seam allowance is not pictured in the construction steps.
- When adjacent pieces are divided with a gray line, use the same fabric.
- Always press the seam allowance in the direction indicated by the arrows.
- The • marks to stop sewing at the seam allowance.

36 Rabbit

A profile view lends this rabbit a dignified air. Use the soft color palette featured in the block pictured below to create a chic-looking rabbit, or opt for bright, patterned fabrics to craft a kid-friendly bunny.

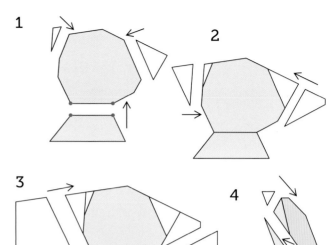

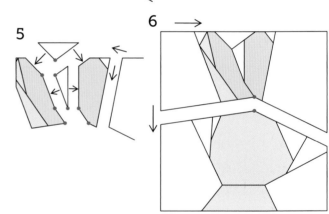

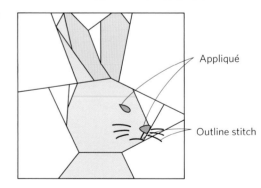

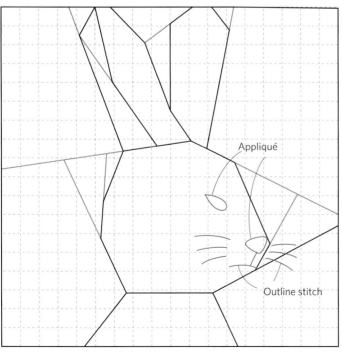

Appliqué

Outline stitch

* When cutting your fabric, add ¼" (0.6 cm) seam allowance around each patchwork piece. Seam allowance is not pictured in the construction steps.
* When adjacent pieces are divided with a gray line, use the same fabric.
* Always press the seam allowance in the direction indicated by the arrows.
* The • marks to stop sewing at the seam allowance.

CONSTRUCTION STEPS

37 Butterfly

I've seen numerous butterfly patchwork patterns, so I wanted to offer quilters a fresh take on a traditional motif. I decided to design this butterfly with large wings that stretch to the very edge of the block. After piecing the block together, I used outline stitch to add the antenna.

1

2

3

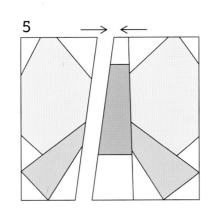

Follow same process to make the right wing

4

5

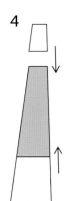

6

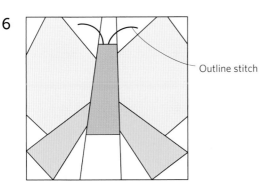

Outline stitch

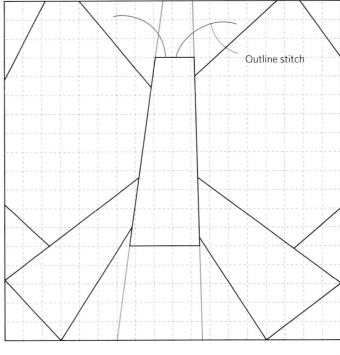

Outline stitch

❖ When cutting your fabric, add ¼" (0.6 cm) seam allowance around each patchwork piece. Seam allowance is not pictured in the construction steps.

❖ When adjacent pieces are divided with a gray line, use the same fabric.

❖ Always press the seam allowance in the direction indicated by the arrows.

38 Dragonfly

This majestic dragonfly was created with a combination of patchwork and appliqué techniques. When selecting fabric, I chose a light-colored checkered print for the wings to give them a transparent look and a green nature-themed print for the background to make the dragonfly look as if he is soaring among the plants.

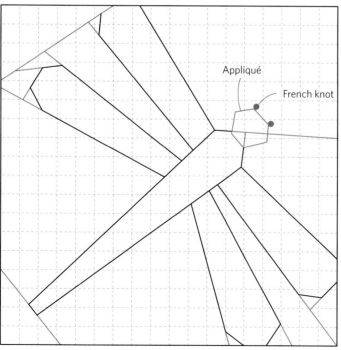

Appliqué

French knot

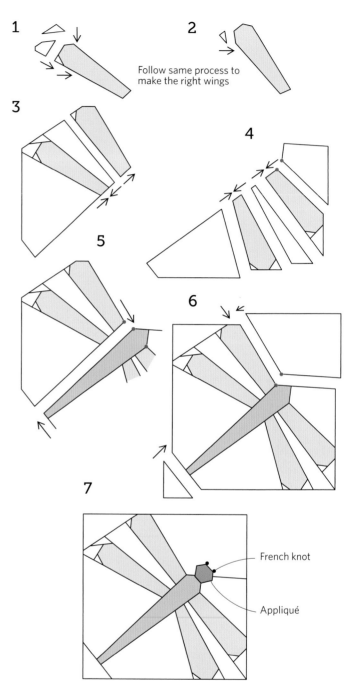

Follow same process to make the right wings

French knot

Appliqué

* When cutting your fabric, add ¼" (0.6 cm) seam allowance around each patchwork piece. Seam allowance is not pictured in the construction steps.
* When adjacent pieces are divided with a gray line, use the same fabric.
* Always press the seam allowance in the direction indicated by the arrows.
* The • marks to stop sewing at the seam allowance.

CONSTRUCTION STEPS

Beetle

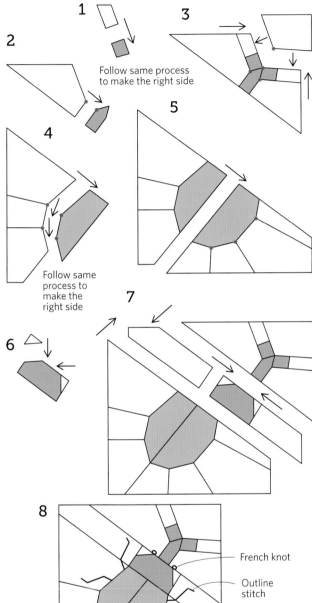

Follow same process to make the right side

Follow same process to make the right side

French knot

Outline stitch

As the most common insect, beetles are popular among children. I used an acorn print for the background fabric of this block to make the beetle appear in his natural habitat. Please note that the back wing pieces are not symmetrical. This block is used for the Beetle Pouch project shown on page 88.

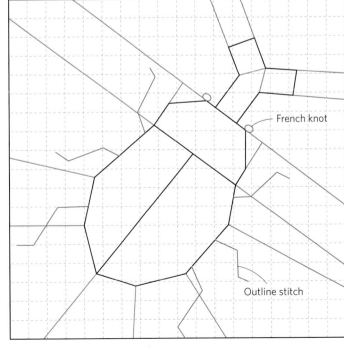

French knot

Outline stitch

❖ When cutting your fabric, add ¼" (0.6 cm) seam allowance around each patchwork piece. Seam allowance is not pictured in the construction steps.

❖ When adjacent pieces are divided with a gray line, use the same fabric.

❖ Always press the seam allowance in the direction indicated by the arrows.

❖ The • marks to stop sewing at the seam allowance.

Beetle Pouch

This pouch is designed with nature lovers in mind. Start with the Beetle block on page 87, then embellish it with an appliquéd tree. The tree trunk is made with bias binding and creates a hidden pocket perfect for storing secret treasures.

MATERIALS FOR BEETLE POUCH

Patchwork and appliqué fabric: Assorted scraps

Front fabric: 9¾" × 11¾" (25 × 30 cm) acorn print fabric

Back fabric: 7⅞" × 9¾" (20 × 25 cm) brown checkered fabric

Backing/lining fabric: 15¾" × 19¾" (40 × 50 cm)

Batting: 9¾" × 15¾" (25 × 40 cm)

Binding:

  For front opening: One 1⅜" × 15¾" (3.5 × 40 cm) wood grain print bias strip

  For pouch opening: One 1⅜" × 15¾" (3.5 × 40 cm) brown checkered bias strip

  For seam allowances: One 1³⁄₁₆" × 15¾" (3 × 40 cm) bias strip

Piping: One 1" × 15¾" (2.5 × 40 cm) dark brown striped bias strip

Piping cord: 15¾" (40 cm) of ⅛" (0.3 cm) diameter piping cord

Zippers:

  For front opening: One 4" (10 cm) long zipper

  For pouch opening: One 6" (15 cm) long zipper

Beads: One 2" (5 cm) long leaf-shaped bead and one ⁷⁄₁₆" (1.2 cm) diameter round bead

Leather cord: 7⅞" (20 cm) of ¹⁄₁₆" (0.2 cm) diameter leather cord

Embroidery floss: 6-strand embroidery floss in black

LAYOUT DIAGRAM

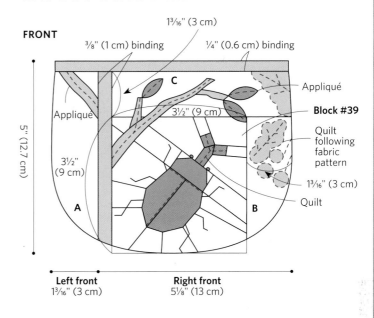

FRONT

1³⁄₁₆" (3 cm)

⅜" (1 cm) binding

¼" (0.6 cm) binding

Appliqué

Appliqué

Block #39

Quilt following fabric pattern

1³⁄₁₆" (3 cm)

Quilt

5" (12.7 cm)

3½" (9 cm)

3½" (9 cm)

A

B

C

Left front
1³⁄₁₆" (3 cm)

Right front
5⅛" (13 cm)

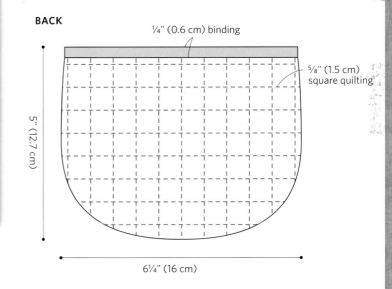

BACK

¼" (0.6 cm) binding

⅝" (1.5 cm) square quilting

5" (12.7 cm)

6¼" (16 cm)

CUTTING INSTRUCTIONS

Seam allowance is not included. Add ¼" (0.6 cm) seam allowance to all piece edges.

Trace and cut out the templates on Pattern Sheet A and the Block #39 template on page 87. Cut out the pieces following the instructions listed on the templates.

✤ Stitch in the ditch along all patchwork pieces.
✤ Sew using ¼" (0.6 cm) seam allowance, unless otherwise noted.

MAKE THE BACK

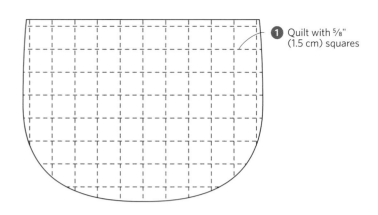

1. Cut the batting and lining slightly larger than the back. Layer the back, batting, and lining. Quilt with ⅝" (1.5 cm) squares.

❶ Quilt with ⅝" (1.5 cm) squares

MAKE THE LEFT FRONT

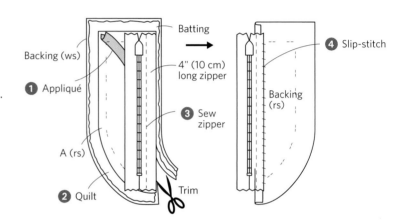

1. Appliqué the tree branch onto piece A.

2. Cut the batting and backing slightly larger than piece A. To make the left front, layer piece A, batting, and backing. Quilt, following the fabric pattern.

3. With right sides together, sew one side of the 4" (10 cm) long zipper to the left front. Trim the excess seam allowance and zipper length, if necessary.

4. Fold back the zipper seam allowance and slip-stitch to the backing.

Backing (ws) · Batting · ❶ Appliqué · A (rs) · ❷ Quilt · 4" (10 cm) long zipper · ❸ Sew zipper · Trim · ❹ Slip-stitch · Backing (rs)

MAKE THE RIGHT FRONT

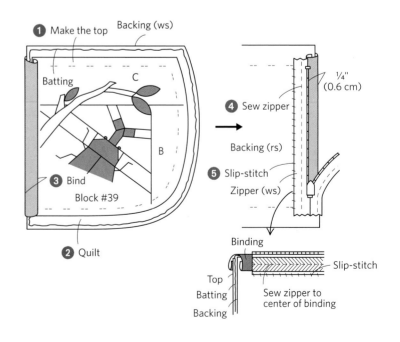

1. Follow the instructions on page 87 to make Block #39. Embroider the legs and eyes. To make the top, sew pieces B and C to Block #39. Appliqué the tree branch and leaves on the top.

2. Cut the batting and backing slightly larger than the assembled top. To make the right front, layer the top, batting, and backing. Quilt, following the fabric pattern.

3. Bind the left edge using the bias strip (refer to page 140 for detailed binding instructions).

4. With right sides together, sew the other side of the zipper to the right front.

5. Fold back the zipper seam allowance and slip-stitch to the backing.

❶ Make the top · Backing (ws) · Batting · C · B · ❸ Bind · Block #39 · ❷ Quilt · ¼" (0.6 cm) · ❹ Sew zipper · Backing (rs) · ❺ Slip-stitch · Zipper (ws) · Binding · Top · Batting · Backing · Slip-stitch · Sew zipper to center of binding

MAKE THE POCKET LINING

1 Align the two pocket linings with right sides facing out.

2 Align pocket linings with the wrong side of the front and baste.

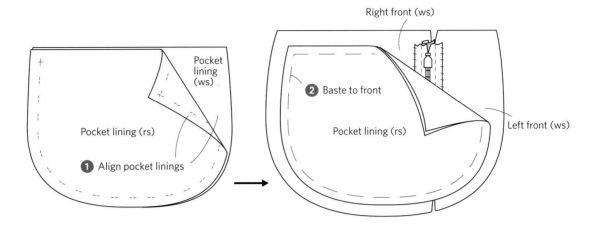

BIND THE POUCH OPENING

1 With right sides together, sew the bias strip to the front.

2 Trim the seam allowances to ¼" (0.6 cm).

3 Wrap the bias strip around the seam allowances and slip-stitch to the pocket lining.

4 Repeat steps 1–3 to bind the back.

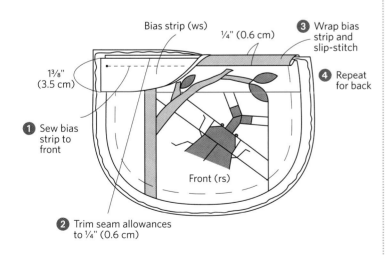

INSTALL THE ZIPPER

1 Baste the back along the finishing line.

2 With right sides together, sew one side of the 6" (15 cm) long zipper to the front and one side to the back. Trim excess zipper length, if necessary.

3 Fold back the zipper seam allowance and slip-stitch to the lining.

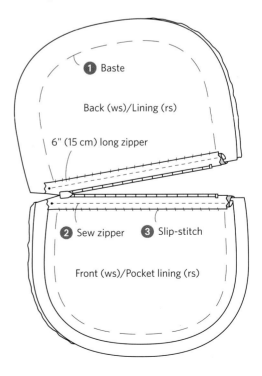

INSTALL THE PIPING AND SEW THE POUCH TOGETHER

1. Fold the piping bias strip in half with the piping cord sandwiched in between. Sew the bias strip close to the cord using a ⅛" (0.3 cm) seam allowance.

2. Baste the piping to the right side of the back along the finishing line. Trim the excess piping.

3. Align the front and back with right sides together and sew along the finishing line.

FINISH THE SEAM ALLOWANCES

1. With right sides together, sew the bias strip to the lining.

2. Trim the excess batting and backing seam allowances to ¼" (0.6 cm).

3. Wrap the bias strip around the seam allowances and slip-stitch to the lining.

4. At the top, fold the raw edges of the bias strip under and slip-stitch, covering the zipper ends.

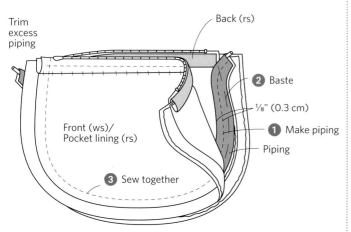

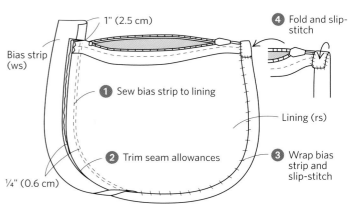

ATTACH THE ZIPPER CHARMS TO FINISH THE POUCH

1. Thread a 4" (10 cm) long leather cord through the leaf-shaped bead.

2. Tie the leather cord to the zipper pull at the pouch opening, trim the excess, and glue the ends together.

3. Tie a 4" (10 cm) long leather cord to the zipper pull at the front opening.

4. Thread the leather cord through the round bead, knot, trim the excess, and glue the ends together.

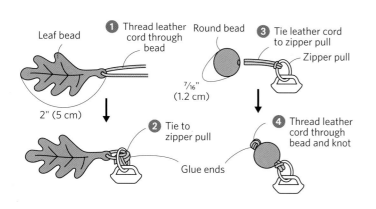

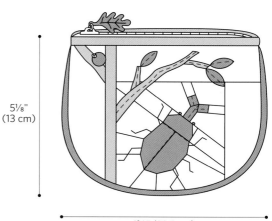

CONSTRUCTION STEPS

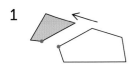

1

2

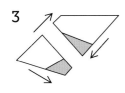

3

4

5

6

7

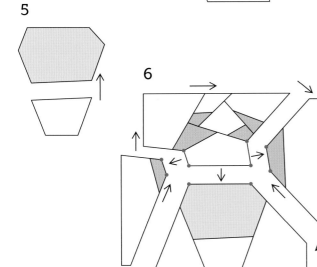

French knot

Outline
stitch

40 Crab

This bright red crustacean stands out on a sandy beach-colored background. The background fabric is even printed with stars, suggesting the presence of starfish. Use outline stitch to make the crab's legs, positioning two stitches next to each other to make the legs thicker at the base.

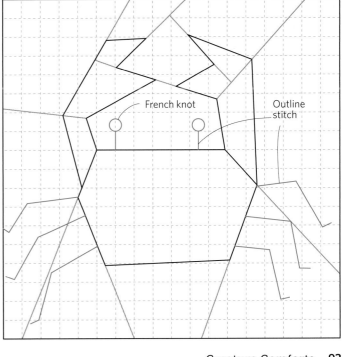

French knot

Outline
stitch

✤ When cutting your fabric, add ¼" (0.6 cm) seam allowance around each patchwork piece. Seam allowance is not pictured in the construction steps.

✤ When adjacent pieces are divided with a gray line, use the same fabric.

✤ Always press the seam allowance in the direction indicated by the arrows.

✤ The • marks to stop sewing at the seam allowance.

41 Blowfish

This block was inspired by the green polka dot fabric—as soon as I saw it, I thought its color would be perfect to use for a fish motif. I chose to design a block featuring a blowfish—one of the world's most fascinating animals!

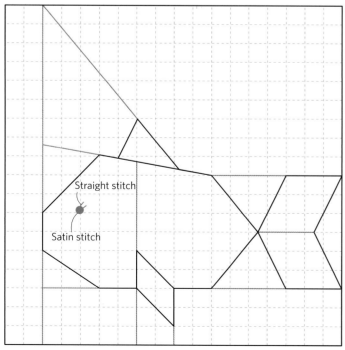

CONSTRUCTION STEPS

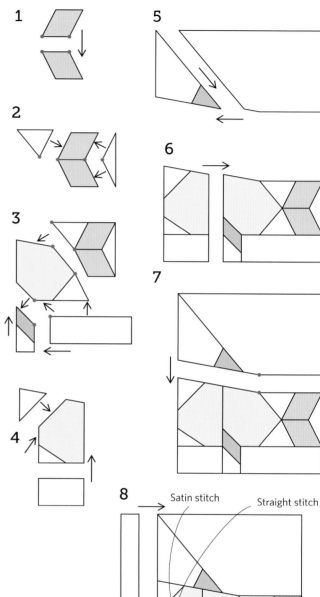

❖ When cutting your fabric, add ¼" (0.6 cm) seam allowance around each patchwork piece. Seam allowance is not pictured in the construction steps.

❖ When adjacent pieces are divided with a gray line, use the same fabric.

❖ Always press the seam allowance in the direction indicated by the arrows.

❖ The • marks to stop sewing at the seam allowance.

42 Pike Fish

With its long, slim silhouette, this fish is unmistakably a pike. The dotted background fabric used for this block lends the appearance of water filled with air bubbles.

1

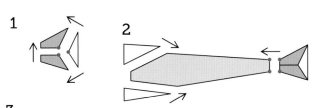

2

3

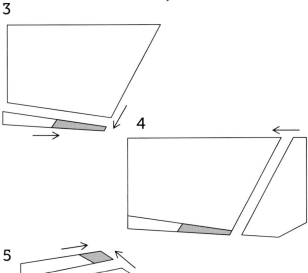

4

5

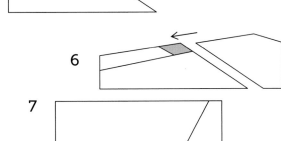

6

7

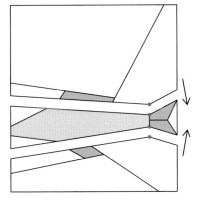

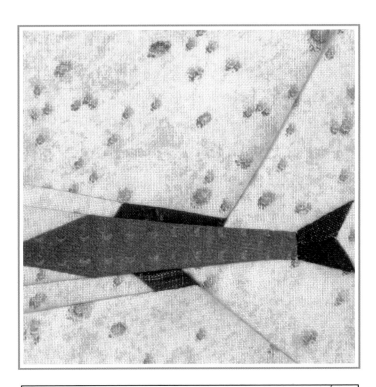

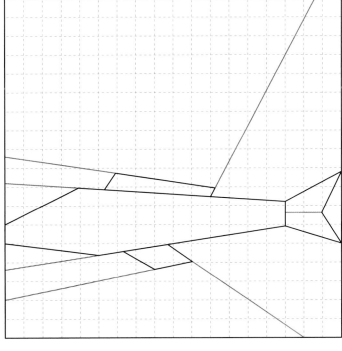

- ✣ When cutting your fabric, add ¼" (0.6 cm) seam allowance around each patchwork piece. Seam allowance is not pictured in the construction steps.
- ✣ When adjacent pieces are divided with a gray line, use the same fabric.
- ✣ Always press the seam allowance in the direction indicated by the arrows.
- ✣ The • marks to stop sewing at the seam allowance.

43 Robot

Made entirely from rectangles, this block works up so fast that you'll feel like a quilting machine! Use it for a quilt, or make it into the Robot Pouch shown on the opposite page.

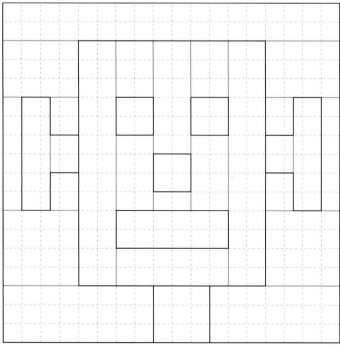

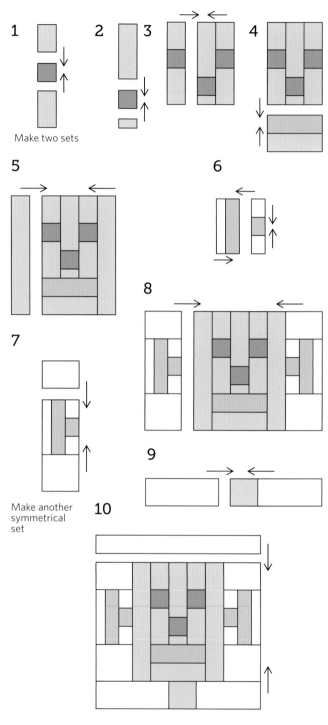

1

2

3

4

Make two sets

5

6

7

Make another symmetrical set

8

9

10

❖ When cutting your fabric, add ¼" (0.6 cm) seam allowance around each patchwork piece. Seam allowance is not pictured in the construction steps.

❖ When adjacent pieces are divided with a gray line, use the same fabric.

❖ Always press the seam allowance in the direction indicated by the arrows.

Robot Pouch

This fun little pouch is perfect for kids, or kids at heart. Assemble the Robot block shown on the opposite page, then add the arms and body with appliqué. Don't forget to embroider the propeller atop his head as a finishing touch!

Instructions on page 98

MATERIALS FOR ROBOT POUCH

Patchwork and appliqué fabric: Assorted scraps

Front fabric: 7⅞" × 9¾" (20 × 25 cm) beige print fabric

Back fabric: 7⅞" × 9¾" (20 × 25 cm) brown checkered fabric

Top gusset fabric: 4" × 9¾" (10 × 25 cm) black and red polka dot fabric

Side gusset fabric: 6" × 7⅞" (15 × 20 cm) brown plaid fabric

Lining fabric: 13¾" × 23⅝" (35 × 60 cm)

Batting: 13¾" × 23⅝" (35 × 60 cm)

Fusible interfacing: 9¾" × 9¾" (25 × 25 cm)

Binding:

For gusset: Two 1⅜" × 9¾" (3.5 × 25 cm) bias strips

For seam allowances: One 1" × 39½" (2.5 × 100 cm) bias strip

Zipper: One 9" (23 cm) long zipper

Beads: Two oval-shaped beads

Zipper charm: One bee-shaped zipper charm

Leather cord: 7⅞" (20 cm) of 1/32" (0.1 cm) diameter leather cord

Stuffing: Polyester/cotton stuffing

Embroidery floss: 6-strand embroidery floss in black, gray, beige, and yellow

LAYOUT DIAGRAM

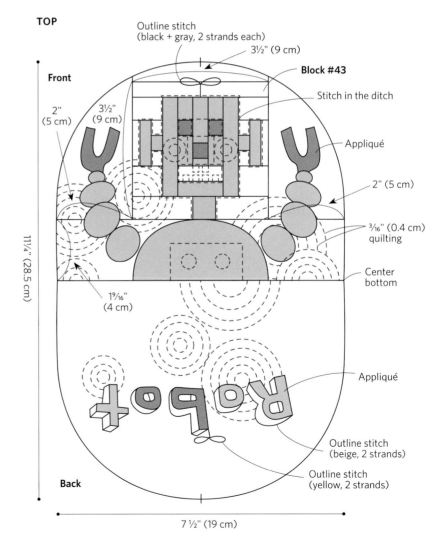

CUTTING INSTRUCTIONS

> Seam allowance is not included. Add ¼" (0.6 cm) seam allowance to all piece edges.

Trace and cut out the templates on Pattern Sheet A and the Block #43 template on page 96. Cut out the pieces following the instructions listed on the templates.

Cut out the following pieces, which do not have templates, according to the measurements below:

✤ **Charm piece (cut 2 without seam allowance):** 1³⁄₁₆" (3 cm) diameter circles of scrap fabric

TOP & SIDE GUSSETS

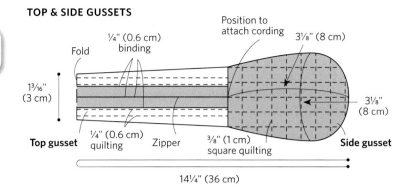

14¼" (36 cm)

CHARM PIECE

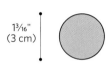

1³⁄₁₆" (3 cm)

> ✤ Stitch in the ditch along all patchwork and appliqué pieces.
> ✤ Sew using ¼" (0.6 cm) seam allowance, unless otherwise noted.

MAKE THE POUCH

1. Follow the instructions on page 96 to make Block #43.

2. Sew the block to the front patchwork pieces.

3. To make the pouch top, align the front and back with right sides together and sew.

4. Appliqué and embroider the top.

5. Cut the batting and lining slightly larger than the assembled top. Layer the top, batting, and lining. Stitch in the ditch around all patchwork and appliqué pieces. Quilt the remaining areas with concentric circles about ³⁄₁₆" (0.4 cm) apart.

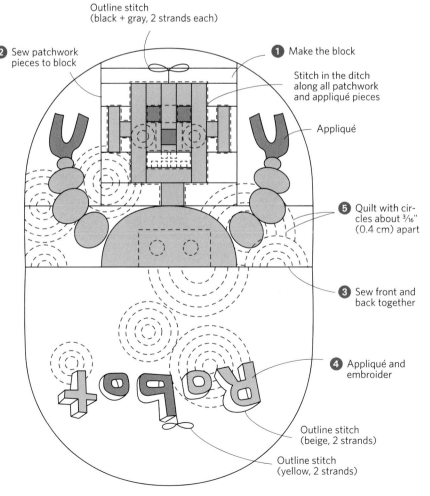

MAKE THE TOP GUSSET

1. Adhere the fusible interfacing to the wrong side of one top gusset lining.

2. Layer the top gusset, batting, and top gusset lining. Baste, then quilt with horizontal lines about ¼" (0.6 cm) apart.

3. Bind one long edge of the top gusset using the bias strip (refer to page 140 for detailed binding instructions).

4. Repeat steps 1–3 to make another top gusset.

5. Align the two top gussets and baste together around the outer edge.

6. Sew the zipper to the top gussets along each side.

7. Slip-stitch the zipper seam allowance to the top gusset lining, trimming excess zipper length, if necessary.

8. Cut the 7⅞" (20 cm) long cord in half. Fold each piece in half. Baste a folded cord to each short end of the top gusset.

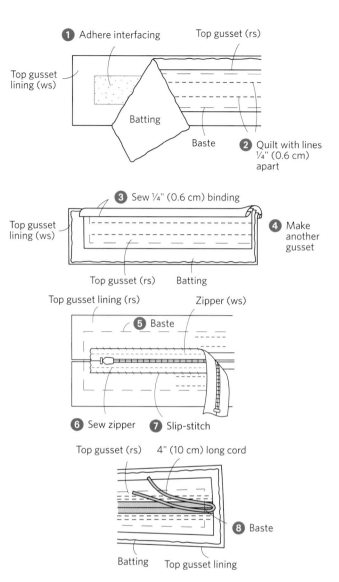

1 Adhere interfacing — Top gusset (rs)
Top gusset lining (ws)
Batting
Baste
2 Quilt with lines ¼" (0.6 cm) apart

3 Sew ¼" (0.6 cm) binding
Top gusset lining (ws)
4 Make another gusset
Top gusset (rs)   Batting

Top gusset lining (rs)   Zipper (ws)
5 Baste
6 Sew zipper   7 Slip-stitch

Top gusset (rs)   4" (10 cm) long cord
8 Baste
Batting   Top gusset lining

MAKE THE SIDE GUSSETS AND ATTACH TO THE TOP GUSSET

1. Layer one side gusset, batting, and side gusset lining. Quilt with ⅜" (1 cm) squares. Repeat to make another side gusset.

2. Align top gusset and side gussets with right sides together and sew.

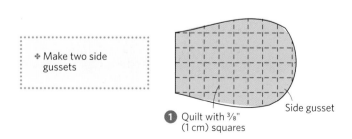

✤ Make two side gussets

1 Quilt with ⅜" (1 cm) squares
Side gusset

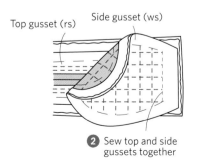

Top gusset (rs)   Side gusset (ws)

2 Sew top and side gussets together

SEW THE POUCH TOGETHER

1 Align the gusset and pouch top with right sides together and sew.

2 Trim the excess seam allowance.

3 Bind the seam allowances with the bias strips (refer to page 73 for detailed binding instructions).

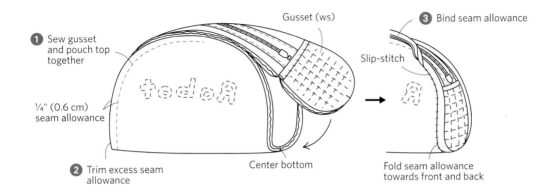

MAKE THE CHARMS TO FINISH THE POUCH

1 Sew around each charm piece with running stitch. Leave long thread tails. Fill with stuffing and pull the thread tails to gather the fabric around the stuffing.

2 Thread an oval bead onto each cord and knot. Insert the knot into the stuffing and tighten the stitches. Knot the thread and trim the excess thread tails.

3 Attach the bee-shaped zipper charm.

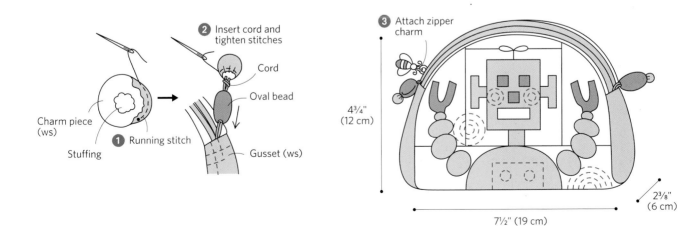

CONSTRUCTION STEPS

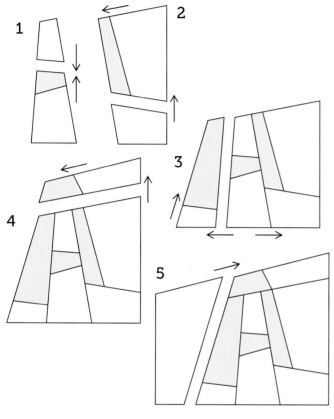

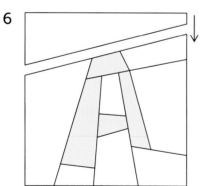

44 Letter A

This collection has you covered from A to Z. Enjoy using the different blocks to add names, initials, and words to your quilts. With all 26 letters of the alphabet included, the possibilities are endless!

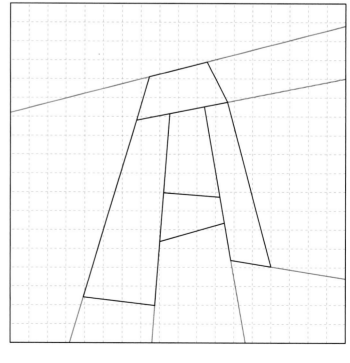

❖ When cutting your fabric, add ¼" (0.6 cm) seam allowance around each patchwork piece. Seam allowance is not pictured in the construction steps.

❖ When adjacent pieces are divided with a gray line, use the same fabric.

❖ Always press the seam allowance in the direction indicated by the arrows.

45 Letter B

When creating these alphabet blocks, I drew the letters free hand. Each letter is composed of several pieces, each with its own unique size and shape. I love the sharp angles used to create the letter B in this block.

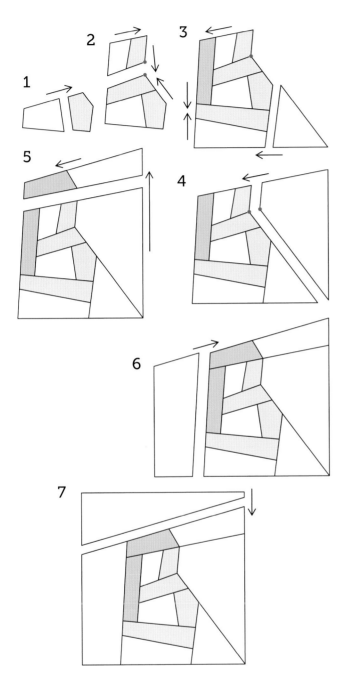

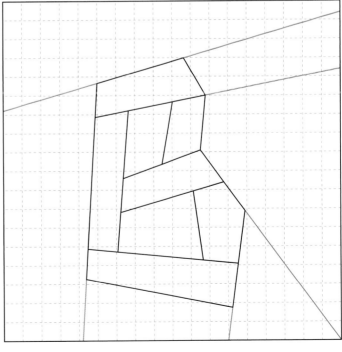

* When cutting your fabric, add ¼" (0.6 cm) seam allowance around each patchwork piece. Seam allowance is not pictured in the construction steps.
* When adjacent pieces are divided with a gray line, use the same fabric.
* Always press the seam allowance in the direction indicated by the arrows.
* The • marks to stop sewing at the seam allowance.

46 Letter C

I've used homespun fabric throughout the alphabet collection because I love working with the natural colors and fun plaids characteristic of this type of fabric. Homespun fabric is yarn-dyed then woven, unlike most fabric, which is printed after being woven.

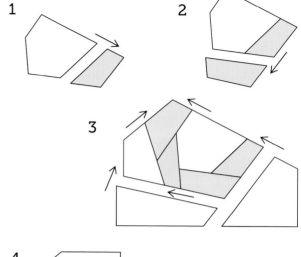

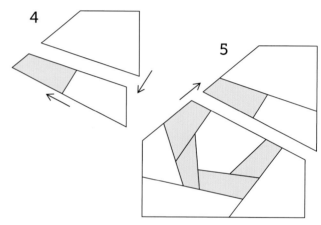

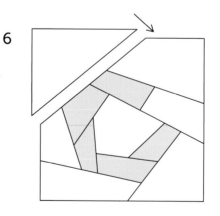

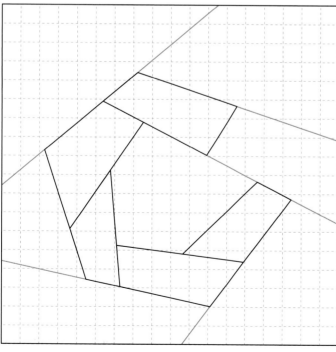

❖ When cutting your fabric, add ¼" (0.6 cm) seam allowance around each patchwork piece. Seam allowance is not pictured in the construction steps.
❖ When adjacent pieces are divided with a gray line, use the same fabric.
❖ Always press the seam allowance in the direction indicated by the arrows.

47 Letter D

This block features a couple of unique elements. First, I used two different materials for the background. I kept the fabric tone the same in order to add a bit of subtle contrast to the block. Second, I positioned the letter D slightly off balance to add visual interest.

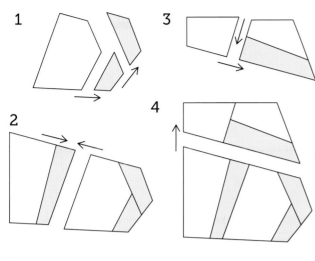

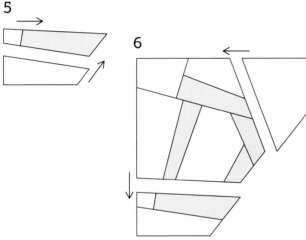

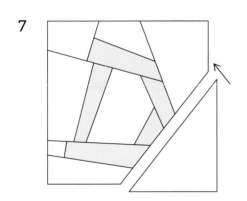

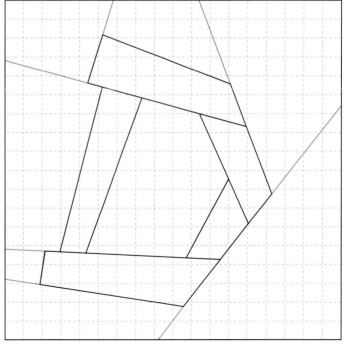

- ❖ When cutting your fabric, add ¼" (0.6 cm) seam allowance around each patchwork piece. Seam allowance is not pictured in the construction steps.
- ❖ When adjacent pieces are divided with a gray line, use the same fabric.
- ❖ Always press the seam allowance in the direction indicated by the arrows.

48 Letter E

I enjoy using patterned fabrics, especially plaids. It is so fun to manipulate the pattern to achieve different looks with the same piece of fabric. When working with checkered or striped fabric, try positioning the lines at different angles within the same block.

1
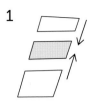

2
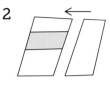

3
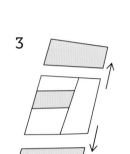

4
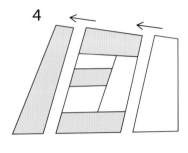

5
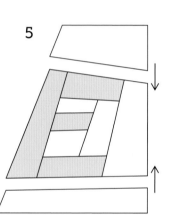

6
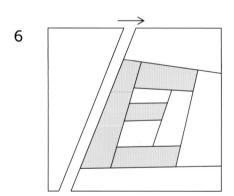

❖ When cutting your fabric, add ¼" (0.6 cm) seam allowance around each patchwork piece. Seam allowance is not pictured in the construction steps.

❖ When adjacent pieces are divided with a gray line, use the same fabric.

❖ Always press the seam allowance in the direction indicated by the arrows.

CONSTRUCTION STEPS

1

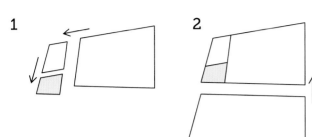

2

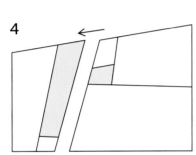

3

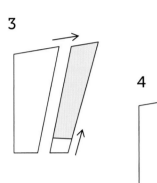

4

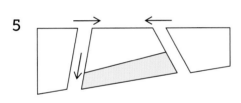

5

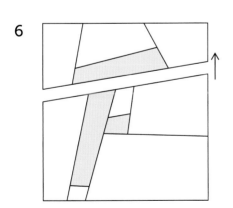

6

49 Letter F

Have fun playing with your fabrics. In this F block, I used a flower print. Consider making a letter quilt to teach a child the alphabet. You could use different prints with images to represent each letter.

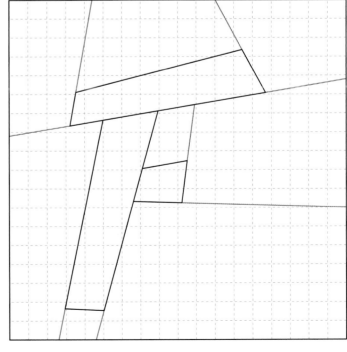

- ❖ When cutting your fabric, add ¼" (0.6 cm) seam allowance around each patchwork piece. Seam allowance is not pictured in the construction steps.
- ❖ When adjacent pieces are divided with a gray line, use the same fabric.
- ❖ Always press the seam allowance in the direction indicated by the arrows.

50 Letter G

Designing this block was one of the most challenging in the collection—creating a curved letter out of straight patchwork pieces is hard work! If you look at the gingham fabric, you will see that some of the background pieces are cut out on the bias.

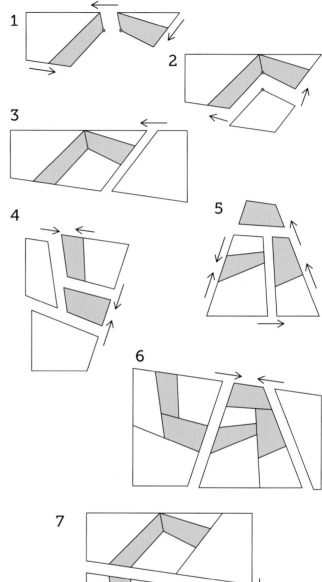

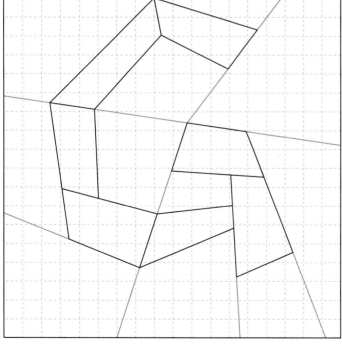

❖ When cutting your fabric, add ¼" (0.6 cm) seam allowance around each patchwork piece. Seam allowance is not pictured in the construction steps.

❖ When adjacent pieces are divided with a gray line, use the same fabric.

❖ Always press the seam allowance in the direction indicated by the arrows.

❖ The • marks to stop sewing at the seam allowance.

51 Letter H

1

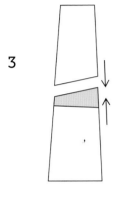

2

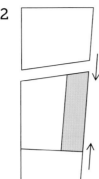

3

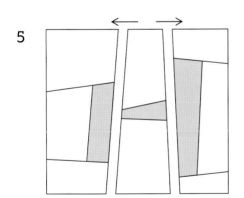

4

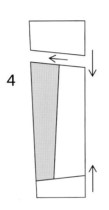

In this block, the two vertical lines forming the letter H are different lengths. This little detail lends an air of playfulness and makes the letter appear hand drawn.

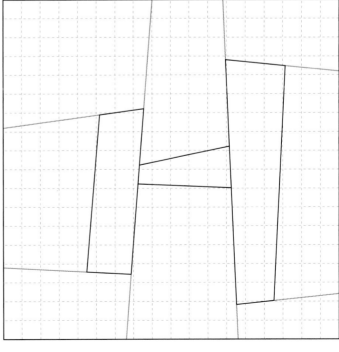

5

❖ When cutting your fabric, add ¼" (0.6 cm) seam allowance around each patchwork piece. Seam allowance is not pictured in the construction steps.

❖ When adjacent pieces are divided with a gray line, use the same fabric.

❖ Always press the seam allowance in the direction indicated by the arrows.

52 Letter I

This I block is very similar to the spool motifs that are featured in the Sewing Corner collection. For this block, I used a wood grain print for the background to emphasize the letter's straight lines.

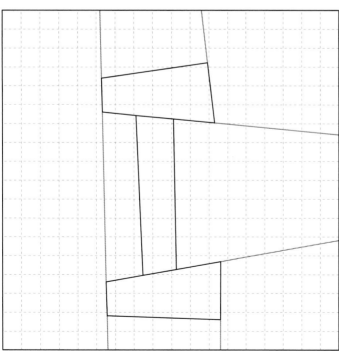

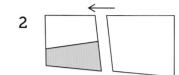

1

2

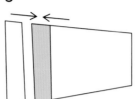

3

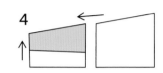

4

5

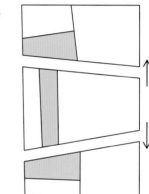

6

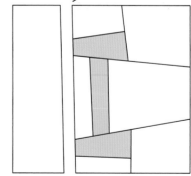

- ❖ When cutting your fabric, add ¼" (0.6 cm) seam allowance around each patchwork piece. Seam allowance is not pictured in the construction steps.
- ❖ When adjacent pieces are divided with a gray line, use the same fabric.
- ❖ Always press the seam allowance in the direction indicated by the arrows.

CONSTRUCTION STEPS

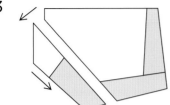

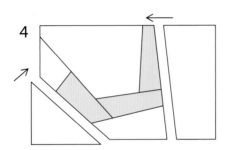

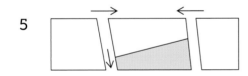

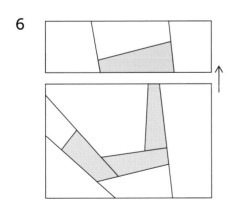

53 Letter J

I really enjoyed selecting the fabric for this block. The letter J is composed of two different green prints, while the background fabric is a *komon* pattern. *Komon* patterns are small-scale, repetitive prints traditionally used in kimonos.

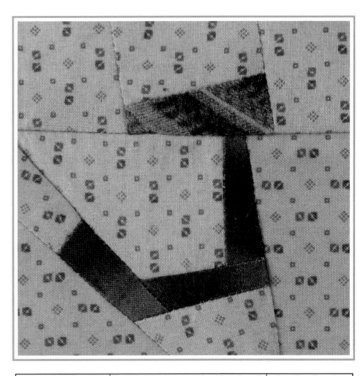

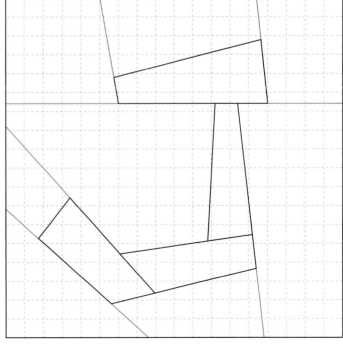

- ❖ When cutting your fabric, add ¼" (0.6 cm) seam allowance around each patchwork piece. Seam allowance is not pictured in the construction steps.
- ❖ When adjacent pieces are divided with a gray line, use the same fabric.
- ❖ Always press the seam allowance in the direction indicated by the arrows.

Letter K

I love using fabric in unexpected ways. The background is composed of only one fabric, but by cutting the pieces out at different angles, I was able to create a dynamic block that looks as if it is composed of several different fabrics.

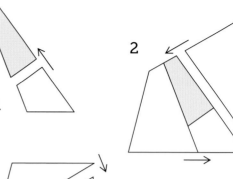

1

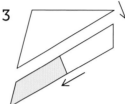

2

3

4

5

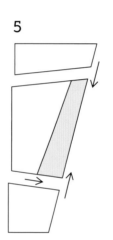

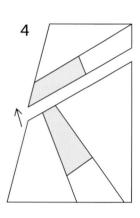

6

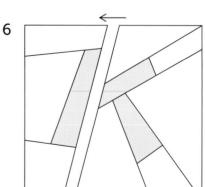

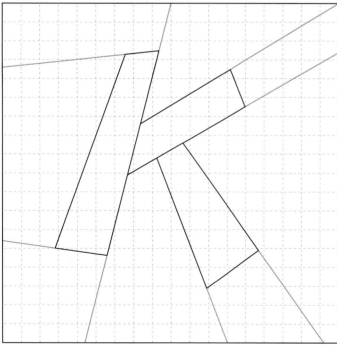

- ❖ When cutting your fabric, add ¼" (0.6 cm) seam allowance around each patchwork piece. Seam allowance is not pictured in the construction steps.
- ❖ When adjacent pieces are divided with a gray line, use the same fabric.
- ❖ Always press the seam allowance in the direction indicated by the arrows.

55 Letter L

The background for this L block is made up of a couple different prints. When combining multiple patterns within the same project, keep in mind that you can create harmony by using fabrics with the same tone, such as the beige used in these fabrics.

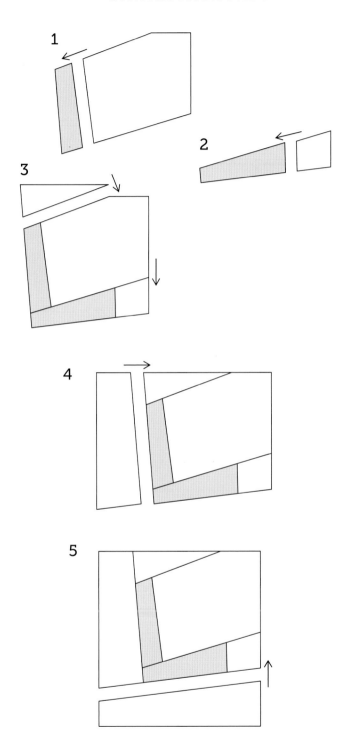

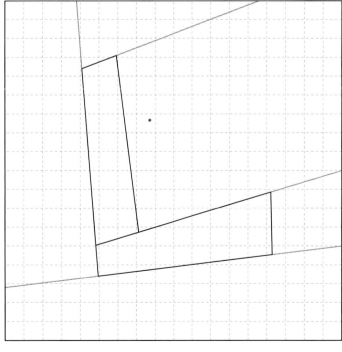

* When cutting your fabric, add ¼" (0.6 cm) seam allowance around each patchwork piece. Seam allowance is not pictured in the construction steps.
* When adjacent pieces are divided with a gray line, use the same fabric.
* Always press the seam allowance in the direction indicated by the arrows.

56 Letter M

When making this block, sew the pieces together carefully to create the pointed, mountain-like tips characteristic of the letter M.

CONSTRUCTION STEPS

1
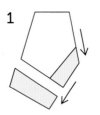

2
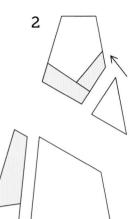

3
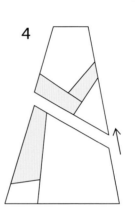

4

5
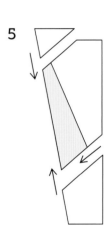

6
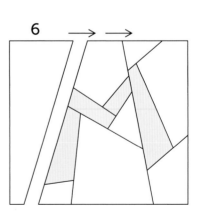

* When cutting your fabric, add ¼" (0.6 cm) seam allowance around each patchwork piece. Seam allowance is not pictured in the construction steps.
* When adjacent pieces are divided with a gray line, use the same fabric.
* Always press the seam allowance in the direction indicated by the arrows.

CONSTRUCTION STEPS

57 Letter N

I think this block is one of the most chic in the entire collection. I designed the letter N with sharp angles and used a modern beige and brown color scheme for a contemporary look.

1
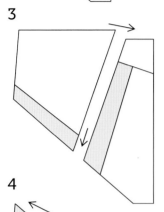

2
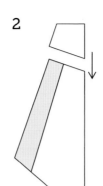

3
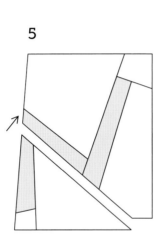

4

5

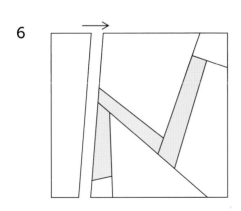

6
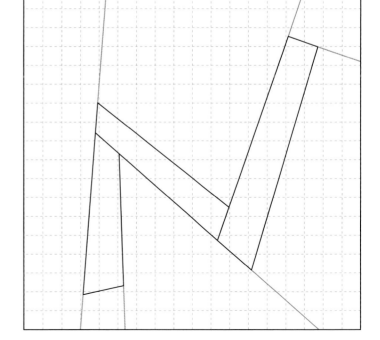

- ✤ When cutting your fabric, add ¼" (0.6 cm) seam allowance around each patchwork piece. Seam allowance is not pictured in the construction steps.
- ✤ When adjacent pieces are divided with a gray line, use the same fabric.
- ✤ Always press the seam allowance in the direction indicated by the arrows.

58 Letter O

Although this block is more simplistic than some of the other letters, it includes a few special details. First, the high color contrast between the moss green and beige makes the letter O stand out. Second, I divided the background into many pieces to add visual interest.

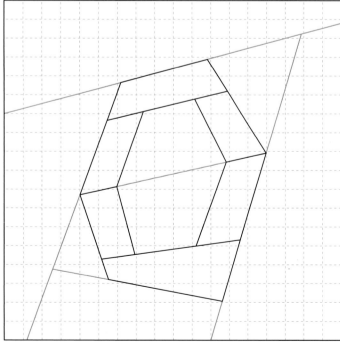

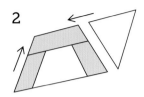
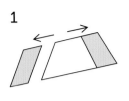
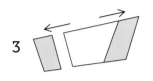
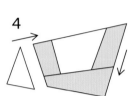
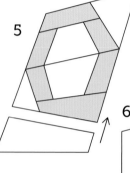
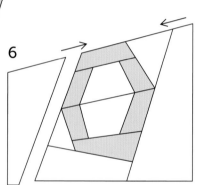

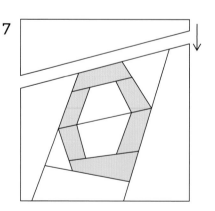

❖ When cutting your fabric, add ¼" (0.6 cm) seam allowance around each patchwork piece. Seam allowance is not pictured in the construction steps.

❖ When adjacent pieces are divided with a gray line, use the same fabric.

❖ Always press the seam allowance in the direction indicated by the arrows.

CONSTRUCTION STEPS

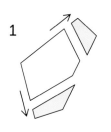

1

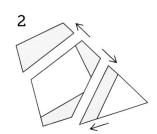

2

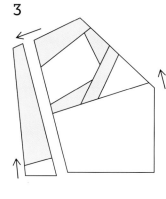

3

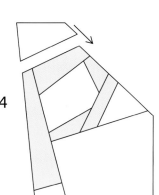

4

For this block, I continued to experiment with color contrast, pairing a soft blue-gray print with a black plaid. The dark color scheme and the high color contrast catch your attention and make a strong impression.

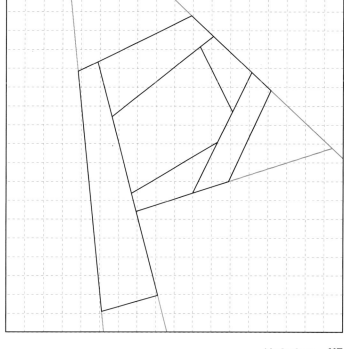

5

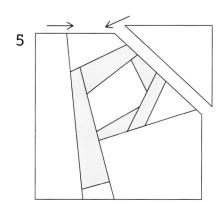

* When cutting your fabric, add ¼" (0.6 cm) seam allowance around each patchwork piece. Seam allowance is not pictured in the construction steps.
* When adjacent pieces are divided with a gray line, use the same fabric.
* Always press the seam allowance in the direction indicated by the arrows.

60 Letter Q

This block contains several fun elements. I used three fabrics, each with a different color, pattern, and texture. Combining woven and print fabrics within the same block adds dimension.

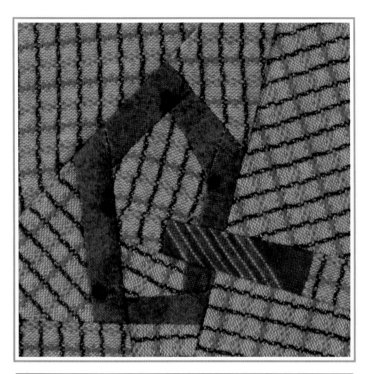

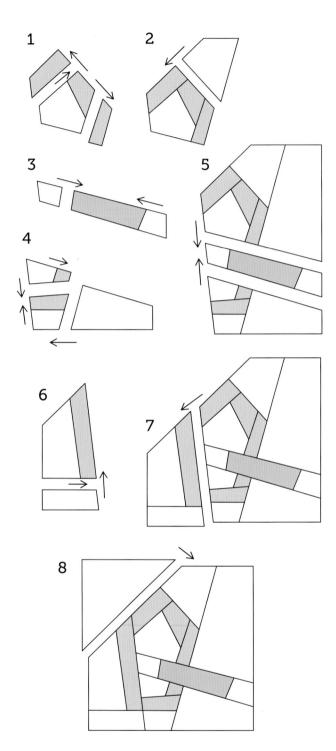

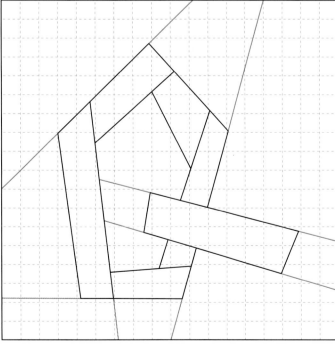

- ❖ When cutting your fabric, add ¼" (0.6 cm) seam allowance around each patchwork piece. Seam allowance is not pictured in the construction steps.
- ❖ When adjacent pieces are divided with a gray line, use the same fabric.
- ❖ Always press the seam allowance in the direction indicated by the arrows.

61 Letter R

This collection features a lot of plaid and checkered fabrics, so I made an effort to design a few blocks with other prints in mind, such as the stripes, dots, and batiks showcased in this motif. I love the way a block can use different prints but be united by the same color scheme.

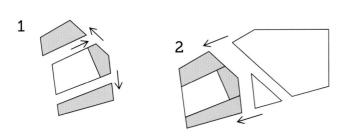

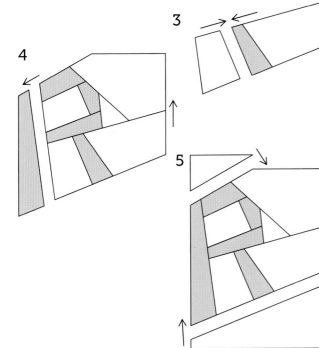

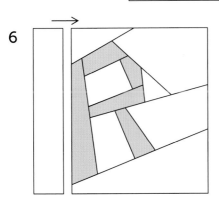

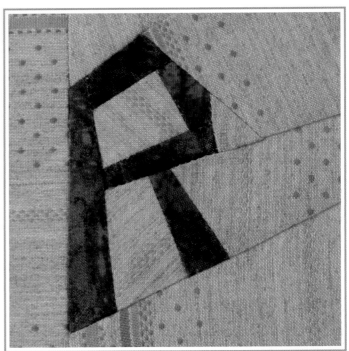

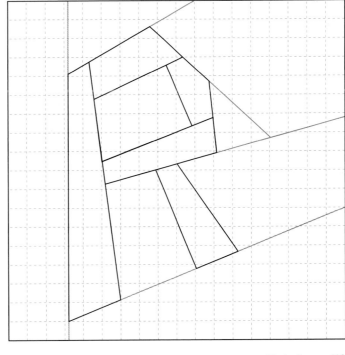

- When cutting your fabric, add ¼" (0.6 cm) seam allowance around each patchwork piece. Seam allowance is not pictured in the construction steps.
- When adjacent pieces are divided with a gray line, use the same fabric.
- Always press the seam allowance in the direction indicated by the arrows.

62 Letter S

In this block, many small pieces are sewn together in order to create the characteristic curves of the letter S, as well as the background. Because this block is divided into so many pieces, it is best suited for small prints rather than large-scale designs.

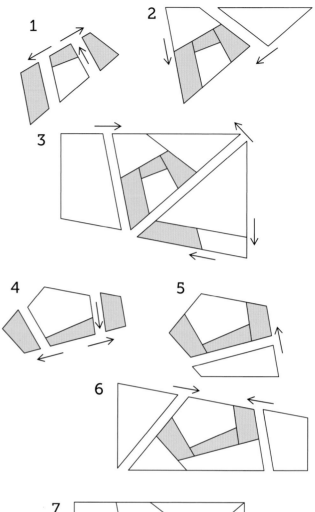

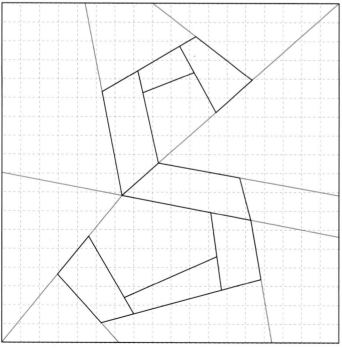

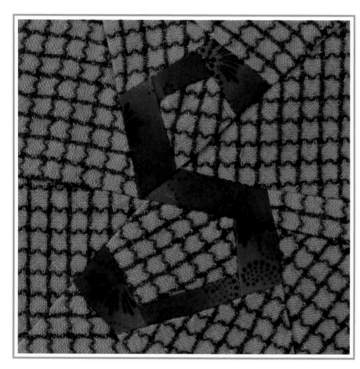

* When cutting your fabric, add ¼" (0.6 cm) seam allowance around each patchwork piece. Seam allowance is not pictured in the construction steps.
* When adjacent pieces are divided with a gray line, use the same fabric.
* Always press the seam allowance in the direction indicated by the arrows.

CONSTRUCTION STEPS

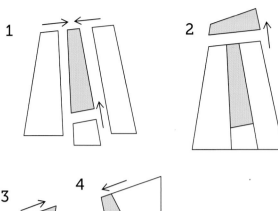

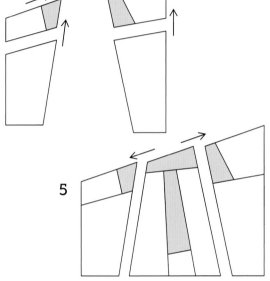

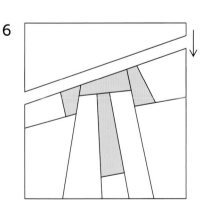

This is a very simple letter to make, so I added some style with the small angled pieces at the top. This beige and blue color scheme is one of my favorites—I find it very refreshing!

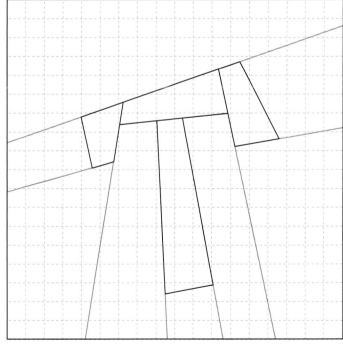

- ✥ When cutting your fabric, add ¼" (0.6 cm) seam allowance around each patchwork piece. Seam allowance is not pictured in the construction steps.
- ✥ When adjacent pieces are divided with a gray line, use the same fabric.
- ✥ Always press the seam allowance in the direction indicated by the arrows.

64 Letter U

Rather than creating a traditionally curved U, I designed this block to be asymmetrical and slightly off balance. I think these features make the block more unique.

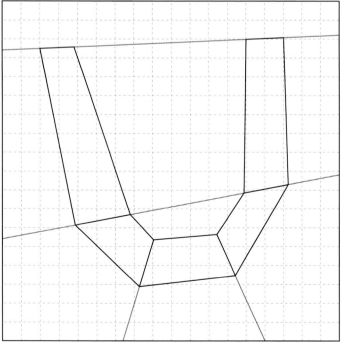

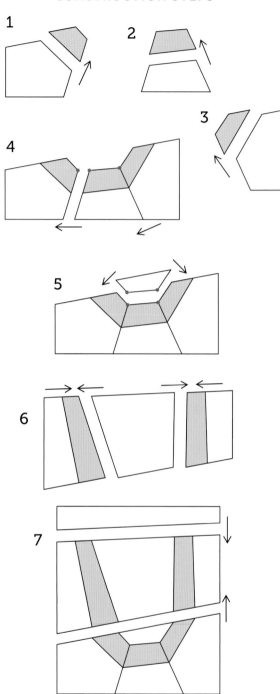

❖ When cutting your fabric, add ¼" (0.6 cm) seam allowance around each patchwork piece. Seam allowance is not pictured in the construction steps.

❖ When adjacent pieces are divided with a gray line, use the same fabric.

❖ Always press the seam allowance in the direction indicated by the arrows.

❖ The • marks to stop sewing at the seam allowance.

CONSTRUCTION STEPS

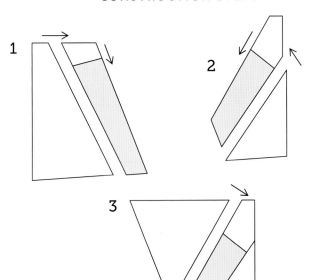

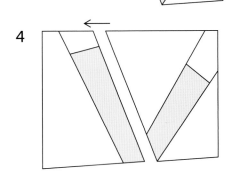

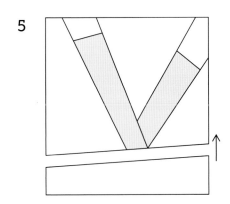

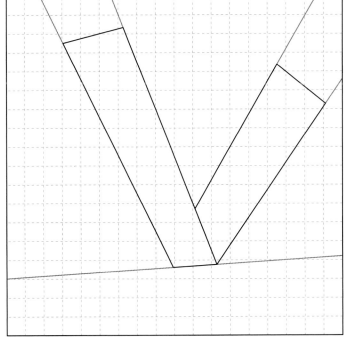

65 Letter V

The bold letter V really stands out in this block. The background fabric is nearly the exact opposite of the fabric used for the patchwork V.

❖ When cutting your fabric, add ¼" (0.6 cm) seam allowance around each patchwork piece. Seam allowance is not pictured in the construction steps.

❖ When adjacent pieces are divided with a gray line, use the same fabric.

❖ Always press the seam allowance in the direction indicated by the arrows.

66 Letter W

This block exhibits contrast through its use of color and pattern. The letter W is made from a dark linear fabric, while the background is made from a light floral print. This motif really plays up the contrast between hard and soft.

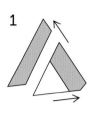
1

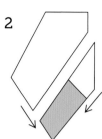
2

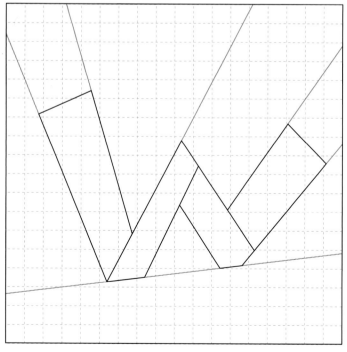

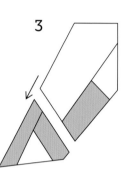
3

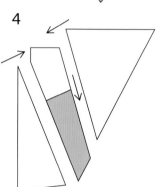
4

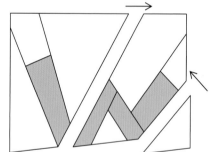
5

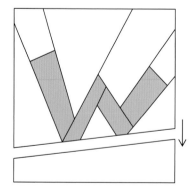
6

❖ When cutting your fabric, add ¼" (0.6 cm) seam allowance around each patchwork piece. Seam allowance is not pictured in the construction steps.

❖ When adjacent pieces are divided with a gray line, use the same fabric.

❖ Always press the seam allowance in the direction indicated by the arrows.

67 Letter X

In this block, the pieces that form the letter X vary in thickness. This was intentional—I wanted the motif to look like a hand-drawn letter rather than a perfectly symmetrical cross.

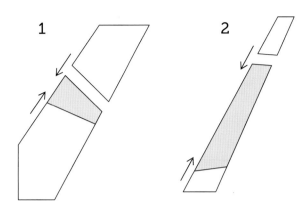

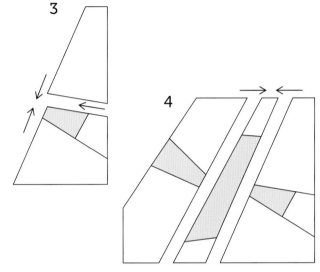

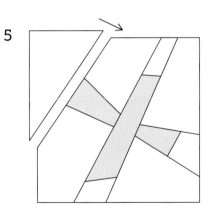

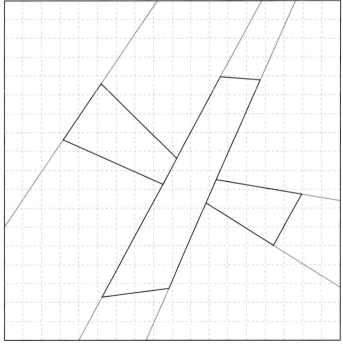

❖ When cutting your fabric, add ¼" (0.6 cm) seam allowance around each patchwork piece. Seam allowance is not pictured in the construction steps.

❖ When adjacent pieces are divided with a gray line, use the same fabric.

❖ Always press the seam allowance in the direction indicated by the arrows.

68 Letter Y

Fabric can have a totally different look depending on the way the pieces are cut. In this block, the background fabric appears as both a stripe and a plaid.

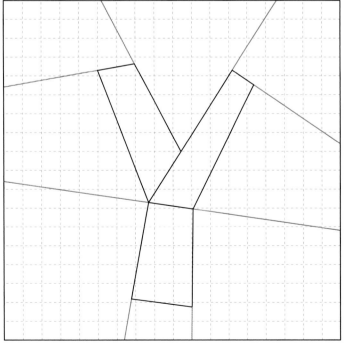

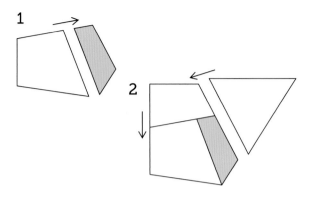

CONSTRUCTION STEPS

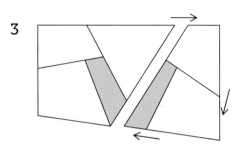

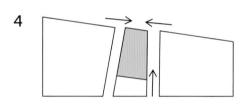

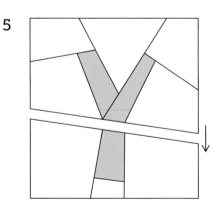

❖ When cutting your fabric, add ¼" (0.6 cm) seam allowance around each patchwork piece. Seam allowance is not pictured in the construction steps.

❖ When adjacent pieces are divided with a gray line, use the same fabric.

❖ Always press the seam allowance in the direction indicated by the arrows.

69 Letter Z

I designed the Z block with a straight, sharp silhouette to lend the last letter of the alphabet an air of finality. I used soft, fuzzy flannel for the background fabric and a brighter print for the letter.

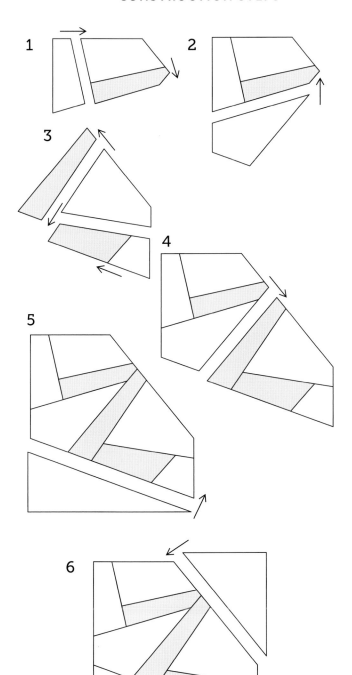

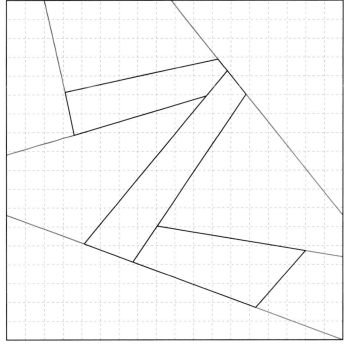

- When cutting your fabric, add ¼" (0.6 cm) seam allowance around each patchwork piece. Seam allowance is not pictured in the construction steps.
- When adjacent pieces are divided with a gray line, use the same fabric.
- Always press the seam allowance in the direction indicated by the arrows.

70 Meandering

Believe it or not, this little block is composed of seven different sizes of squares and rectangles. Use this block to create a stunning geometric quilt—just rotate every other block 90°. This block is also used in the Compass Bag project on page 136.

CONSTRUCTION STEPS

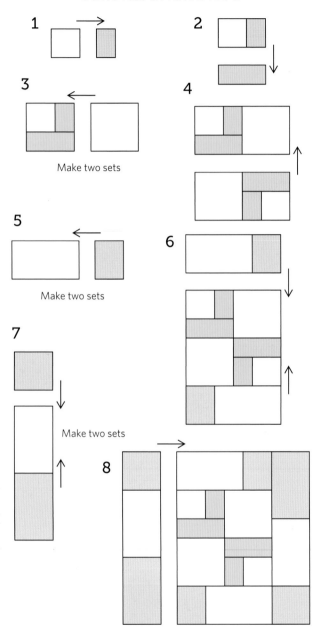

1

2

3

Make two sets

4

5

Make two sets

6

Make two sets

7

8

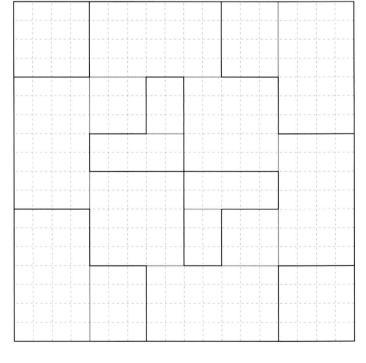

❖ When cutting your fabric, add ¼" (0.6 cm) seam allowance around each patchwork piece. Seam allowance is not pictured in the construction steps.

❖ When adjacent pieces are divided with a gray line, use the same fabric.

❖ Always press the seam allowance in the direction indicated by the arrows.

CONSTRUCTION STEPS

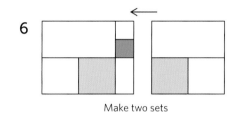

1

2

Make another symmetrical set

3

4

Make four sets

5

6

Make two sets

7

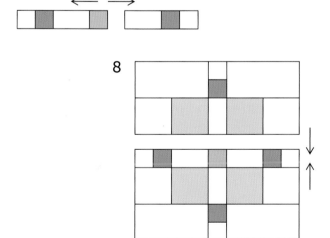

8

For this block, I used a light colored background fabric to make the center design look like it's floating. The green checkerboard fabric tricks the eye and makes the block appear more elaborate than it actually is. This block is featured in the Compass Bag project on page 136.

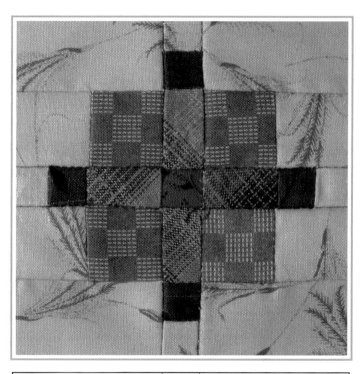

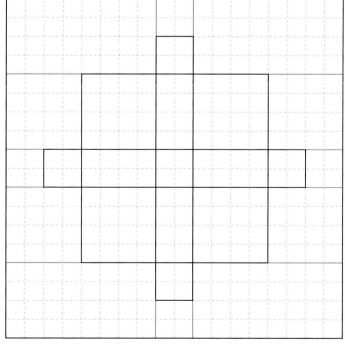

- ✤ When cutting your fabric, add ¼" (0.6 cm) seam allowance around each patchwork piece. Seam allowance is not pictured in the construction steps.
- ✤ When adjacent pieces are divided with a gray line, use the same fabric.
- ✤ Always press the seam allowance in the direction indicated by the arrows.

72 Hexagon Box

This versatile design can be used as photographed here, or rotated at a 90° angle for a completely different look. I love the way the hexagon pieces overlap, making the entire block seem like a jigsaw puzzle. This block is part of the Compass Bag project on page 136.

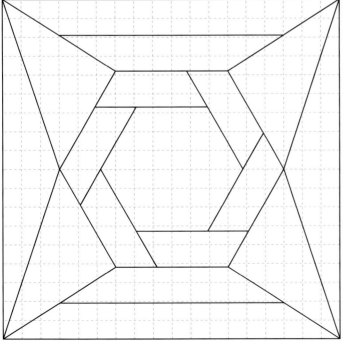

CONSTRUCTION STEPS

1

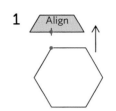

2

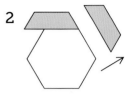

3

4

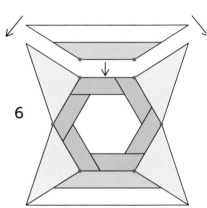

5

Make two sets

6

7

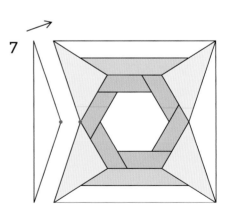

❖ When cutting your fabric, add ¼" (0.6 cm) seam allowance around each patchwork piece. Seam allowance is not pictured in the construction steps.

❖ Always press the seam allowance in the direction indicated by the arrows.

❖ The • marks to stop sewing at the seam allowance.

CONSTRUCTION STEPS

1
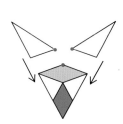

2
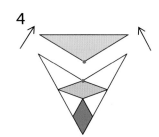

3

4
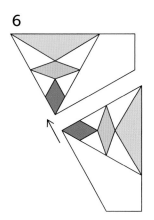

5
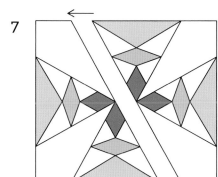

Make
four sets

6

7

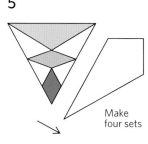

- When cutting your fabric, add ¼" (0.6 cm) seam allowance around each patchwork piece. Seam allowance is not pictured in the construction steps.
- When adjacent pieces are divided with a gray line, use the same fabric.
- Always press the seam allowance in the direction indicated by the arrows.
- The • marks to stop sewing at the seam allowance.

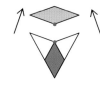

73 Apple Half

To me, this block looks like a cross section of an apple—the small brown diamonds represent the seeds and the beige background fabric represents the fruit. This block is included in the Compass Bag project on page 136.

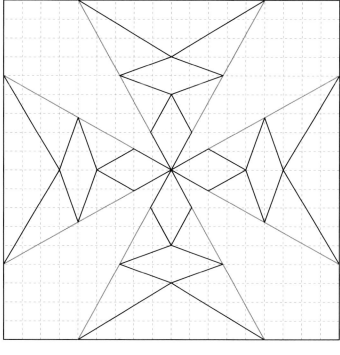

74 Cheerful Compass

This block was created by drawing a circle, then dividing it into many different sections with irregular lines. The round appliqué portion of this block is used in the Compass Bag project on page 136.

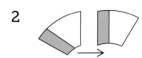

1

2

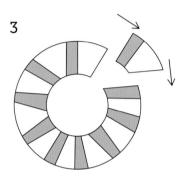

3

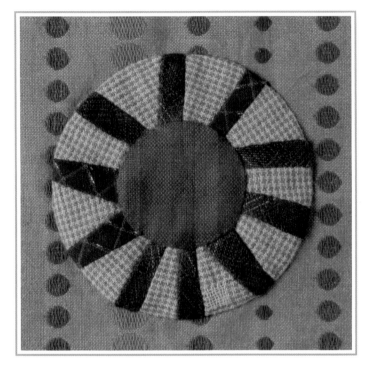

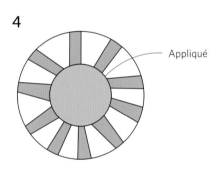

4

Appliqué

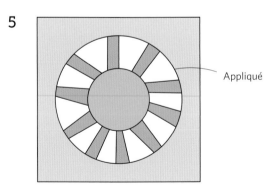

5

Appliqué

* When cutting your fabric, add ¼" (0.6 cm) seam allowance around each patchwork piece. Seam allowance is not pictured in the construction steps.
* Always press the seam allowance in the direction indicated by the arrows.

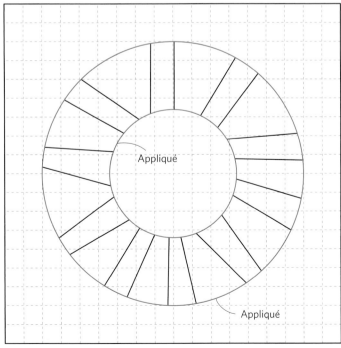

Appliqué

Appliqué

CONSTRUCTION STEPS

75 Star Flower

This design may be simple, but the bold star makes a powerful statement. The star is created by alternating diamonds and triangles. The round appliqué part of this block is used in the Compass Bag project on page 136.

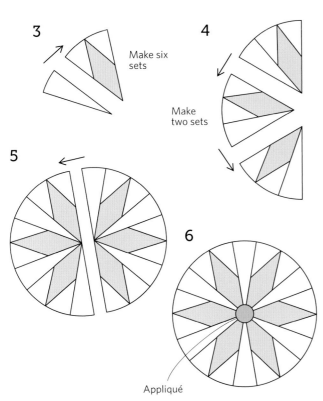

Make six sets

Make two sets

Appliqué

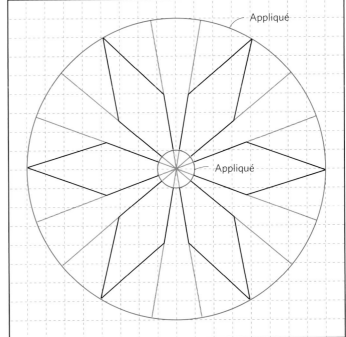

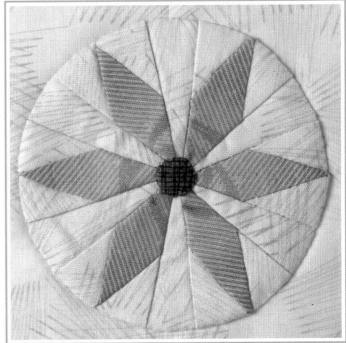

Appliqué

Appliqué

Appliqué

- ❖ When cutting your fabric, add ¼" (0.6 cm) seam allowance around each patchwork piece. Seam allowance is not pictured in the construction steps.
- ❖ When adjacent pieces are divided with a gray line, use the same fabric.
- ❖ Always press the seam allowance in the direction indicated by the arrows.

76 Sunrise Compass

Combining both appliqué and patchwork techniques, this block emphasizes the contrast between curves and straight lines. If the block becomes too bulky after appliquéing, trim the background fabric from the wrong side. This motif is used in the Compass Bag project on page 136.

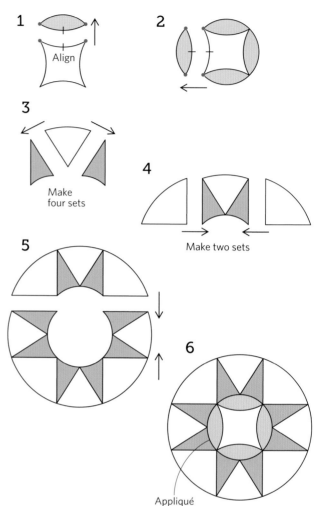

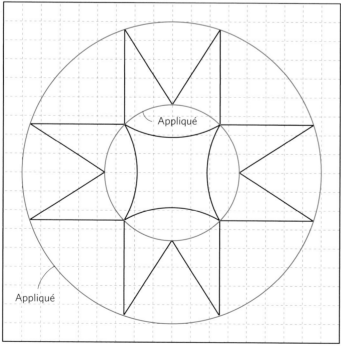

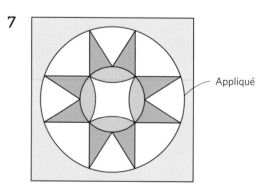

* When cutting your fabric, add ¼" (0.6 cm) seam allowance around each patchwork piece. Seam allowance is not pictured in the construction steps.
* Always press the seam allowance in the direction indicated by the arrows.
* The • marks to stop sewing at the seam allowance.

CONSTRUCTION STEPS

77 Spinning Wheel

Do you love sewing curves? If you answered yes, then this is the perfect block for you! This design features circular layers intersected with a cross. This block is featured in the Compass Bag project on page 136.

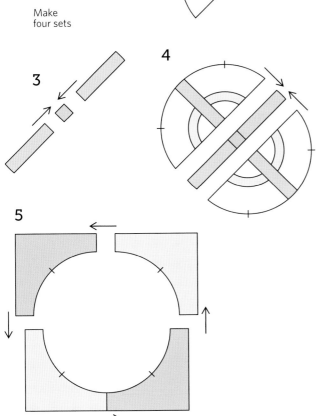

1
Align

Make four sets

2
Make two sets

3

4

5

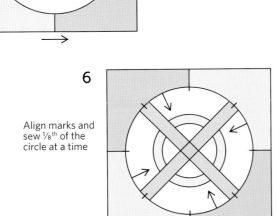

6
Align marks and sew ⅛th of the circle at a time

❖ When cutting your fabric, add ¼" (0.6 cm) seam allowance around each patchwork piece. Seam allowance is not pictured in the construction steps.

❖ Always press the seam allowance in the direction indicated by the arrows.

Compass Bag

This bag is made with eight different blocks that were trimmed into circles and appliquéd.
Feel free to choose your favorite blocks for a customized bag that is truly one-of-a-kind!

Instructions on page 138

MATERIALS FOR COMPASS BAG

Patchwork and appliqué fabric: Assorted scraps

Main fabric: 15¾" × 19¾" (40 × 50 cm) beige print

Accent fabric: 11¾" × 13¾" (30 × 35 cm) light brown plaid fabric

Lining/facing fabric: 27½" × 35½" (70 × 90 cm)

Bottom fabric: 7⅞" × 15¾" (20 × 40 cm) brown plaid fabric

Bottom foundation fabric: 7⅞" × 15¾" (20 × 40 cm)

Binding: One 1" × 19¾" (2.5 × 50 cm) bias strip

Batting: 27½" × 35½" (70 × 90 cm)

Fusible interfacing: 11¾" × 13¾" (30 × 35 cm)

Heavyweight fusible interfacing: 13¾" × 13¾" (35 × 35 cm)

Handle: 23⅝" (60 cm) of 1³⁄₁₆" (3 cm) wide nylon webbing tape

Buckles: Four 1³⁄₁₆" (3 cm) wide oval-shaped buckles

CUTTING INSTRUCTIONS

Seam allowance is not included. Add ¼" (0.6 cm) seam allowance to all piece edges.

Trace and cut out the templates on Pattern Sheet B and the Block #70–#77 templates on pages 128–135. Cut out the pieces following the instructions listed on the templates.

LAYOUT DIAGRAM

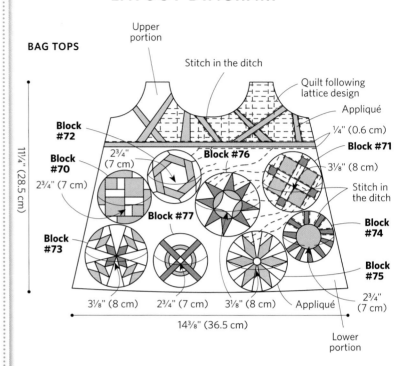

BAG TOPS

11¼" (28.5 cm)

Upper portion
Stitch in the ditch
Quilt following lattice design
Appliqué
¼" (0.6 cm)
Block #72
Block #70
2¾" (7 cm)
2¾" (7 cm)
Block #76
Block #71
3⅛" (8 cm)
Stitch in the ditch
Block #77
Block #73
Block #74
Block #75
3⅛" (8 cm)
2¾" (7 cm)
3⅛" (8 cm)
Appliqué
2¾" (7 cm)
Lower portion
14⅜" (36.5 cm)

FACING

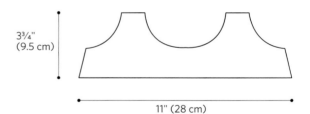

3¾" (9.5 cm)

11" (28 cm)

BOTTOM

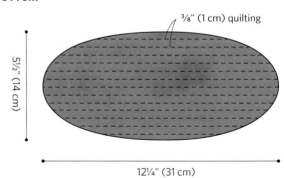

⅜" (1 cm) quilting

5½" (14 cm)

12¼" (31 cm)

❖ Stitch in the ditch along all patchwork and appliqué pieces.

❖ Sew using ¼" (0.6 cm) seam allowance, unless otherwise noted.

MAKE THE BLOCKS AND APPLIQUÉ BAG TOPS

① Follow the instructions on pages 128–135 to make two of Blocks #70–#77. Note: Make only the round portion of Blocks #74–#77. These blocks will not need to be trimmed into shape.

② Make a 2¾" (7 cm) round template and trim the blocks into circles. Make sure to add ¼" (0.6 cm) seam allowance.

③ Baste the circles to the bag tops.

④ Fold the seam allowances under and slip-stitch the circles to the bag tops.

⑤ On the wrong side, trim the excess main fabric behind the circles.

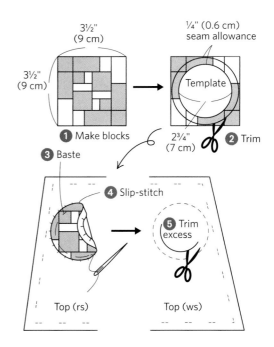

APPLIQUÉ LATTICE DESIGN

① Appliqué the lattice design to the upper portion of bag tops.

② Sew the upper portions to the lower portions of the bag tops.

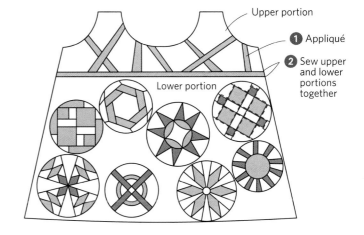

MAKE THE FACINGS

① Adhere fusible interfacing to the wrong side of each facing piece.

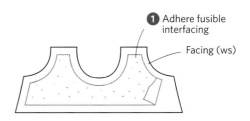

SEW THE FACINGS TO THE BAG TOPS

1 Cut the battings and linings slightly larger than the assembled tops. Layer each top, batting, and lining. Baste. Quilt, as shown in the layout diagram on page 138.

2 Align each facing and top with right sides together and sew together around top edge.

3 Trim seam allowances and clip curves. Turn the facings to the inside.

4 Slip-stitch the facings to the lining.

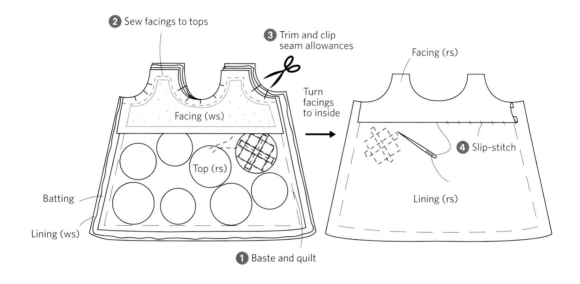

SEW THE BAG TOGETHER

1 Align the two bag tops with right sides together and sew along two sides.

2 Trim the excess seam allowances.

3 With right sides together, sew the bias strips to the seam allowances.

4 Wrap the bias strips around the seam allowances.

5 Slip-stitch the bias strips to the lining.

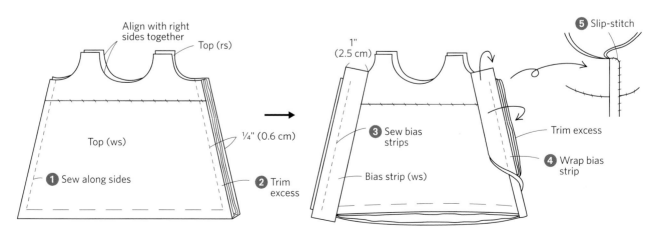

MAKE THE BOTTOM

1 Adhere heavyweight fusible interfacing to the wrong side of the bottom foundation.

2 Layer bottom, batting, and bottom foundation. Baste.

3 Quilt with horizontal lines about ⅜" (1 cm) apart, as shown in the layout diagram on page 138.

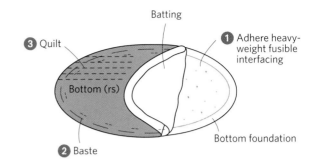

ATTACH THE BOTTOM TO THE BAG

1 Running stitch the bag along the bottom outline and gather into shape.

2 Align the bottom and bag with right sides together and sew.

3 Adhere heavyweight fusible interfacing to the wrong side of the bottom lining.

4 Running stitch the bottom lining and gather into shape.

5 Slip-stitch the bottom lining to the bag lining.

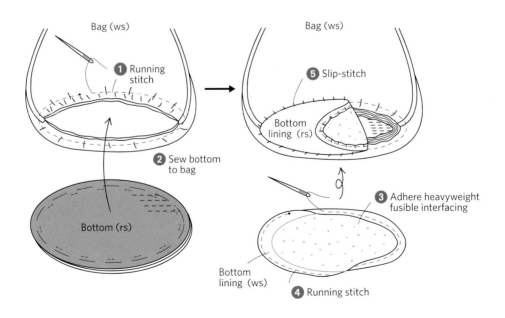

MAKE THE HANDLES

1 Cut the nylon webbing tape into two 11" (28 cm) long pieces. Fold each piece in half widthwise and sew using 4" (10 cm) long seams along the center.

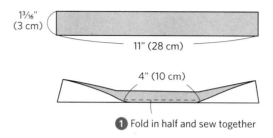

1³⁄₁₆"
(3 cm)

11" (28 cm)

4" (10 cm)

1 Fold in half and sew together

ATTACH THE HANDLES TO THE BAG TO FINISH

1 Thread each handle end through a buckle. Fold the raw edge over, then fold the handle around the buckle.

2 Sew across the handle to secure.

3 Thread the top ⁵⁄₈" (1.5 cm) of the bag through each buckle and fold to the inside of the bag.

4 Sew across bag top to secure.

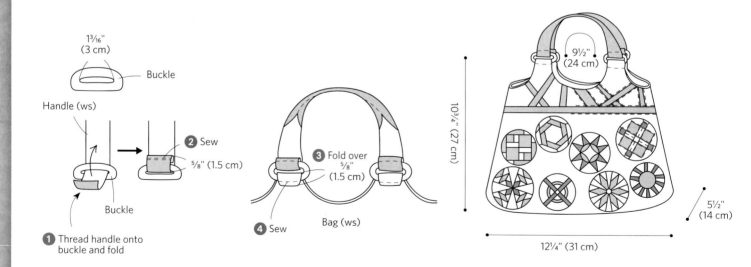

CONSTRUCTION STEPS

1

Make two sets

2

3

4

5

Position this block as shown here, or rotate it to create a vertical diamond...the choice is yours. I used a darker colored fabric for the bottom corners to achieve a sense of balance. This block is used in the Cat & Dog Box project on page 76.

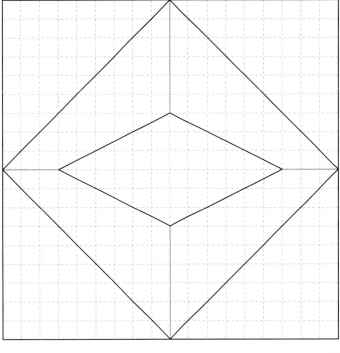

- When cutting your fabric, add ¼" (0.6 cm) seam allowance around each patchwork piece. Seam allowance is not pictured in the construction steps.
- When adjacent pieces are divided with a gray line, use the same fabric.
- Always press the seam allowance in the direction indicated by the arrows.
- The • marks to stop sewing at the seam allowance.

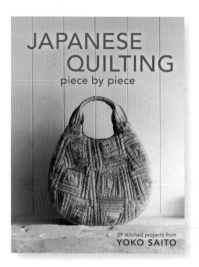

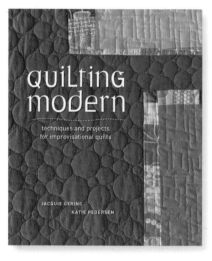